D0291969

3 ISSUES IN ETHICS

3 ISSUES IN ETHICS

John Macquarrie

1817

HARPER & ROW, PUBLISHERS
NEW YORK, EVANSTON, AND LONDON

LIBRARY OF CONGRESS CATALOG CARD NUMBER: 73-109057

To
John Coleman Bennett
President of Union Theological Seminary
New York
1963–70

Contents

Preface		9
1.	THEOLOGY AND ETHICS	11
2.	PROBLEMS OF THE NEW MORALITY	25
3.	ETHICS AND THE NEW MAN	43
4.	RETHINKING NATURAL LAW	82
5.	CONSCIENCE, SIN, AND GRACE	111
6.	HOPE AND THE MORAL DYNAMIC	131
	Notes	147
	Index	155

PREFACE

In these days of specializing it is perhaps something of a risk for one whose competence is in systematic theology to write on the subject of ethics. But none of us is spared from the business of making moral decisions, and so, in turn, from the obligation of ethical reflection. In this book the concern is with some of the basic issues in the relation of theology and ethics, rather than with specific moral problems.

My interest in the subject was stimulated through editing *A Dictionary of Christian Ethics* (S.C.M. Press, London, and Westminster Press, Philadelphia, 1967), a task which brought me into contact with some of the leading Christian moralists of the day. Parts of this book were composed for lecture series, namely, the Whitman Lectures at Nashotah House, March, 1967; the Richards Lectures at the University of Virginia, November, 1967; the Penick Lectures at the University of North Carolina, February, 1969; and the Hughes-Cheong Memorial Lectures at the University of Melbourne, August, 1969. I wish to thank the trustees of these lectureships for their invitations, and also to express thanks for the hospitality of the several institutions.

A summary of Chapter II appeared in *The Nashotah Quarterly Review,* Vol. VII, 1967, and a much abridged version of Chapter III in *Saint Luke's Journal,* Vol. XI, 1967.

Union Theological Seminary   JOHN MACQUARRIE
New York City

1 Theology and Ethics

Men have always had to make moral decisions, and serious-minded people have always engaged in ethical reflection. But today the demand for such ethical reflection has become more insistent, and none of us can escape it. In a rapidly changing world, new techniques and new possibilities thrust themselves upon us. In many cases we can no longer make our decisions according to rules and precedents, because the matters about which we have to decide are unprecedented.

"Science," remarks Harold Hatt, "has made ethical decision-making more significant and also more difficult. Guides for the conduct of life in the horse-and-buggy age are not adequate in the age of high-horsepower cars and space vehicles."[1] The problems created by scientific and technological advance arise at all levels. Techniques of contraception, for instance, raise ethical problems on the personal level, while space exploration and atomic energy raise much vaster problems which are still ethical problems but which affect the entire human race.

Often enough, we do not perceive the ethical dimensions

11

of our activities until they have already become well established. "The disturbing fact," writes Roger Shinn, "is that . . . our society is constantly making decisions, often without knowing what it is doing. We are moving the world toward harmony or destruction, directing people toward prosperity or starvation, offering persons better working opportunities or consigning them to uselessness."[2] These words stress the urgency for ethical reflection, yet they also show how bewildering the situation is.

I do not propose to offer any pretended wisdom on the great substantive moral problems that confront us today, though I shall touch on some of them incidentally and I am writing in constant awareness of them. However, to discuss them in any depth would seem to demand a vast fund of expert knowledge of economics, science, medicine, or whatever other subject might impinge on these problems. The tackling of them must be a cooperative work to which not only ethicists but specialists from all the different fields must make their contributions.

Has a Christian theologian anything to offer? In the past, morality in the Western nations has been closely connected with Christianity. At least, this would be true of personal ethics, though social and international morality has not been obviously influenced by Christian standards. In the increasingly secularized world of today, it might seem that Christian theology has no longer any relevance to ethical questions, and some would claim that its influence in the past has been harmful. Yet even in this secular age there are many persons who look to Christianity for help and who believe that out of its vast store of spiritual understanding and experience (they may be unwilling to acknowledge any "revelation") it still offers resources for resolving our problems.

This book is written with the conviction that Christianity is relevant to our problems and does have something important to say. But this claim is made modestly. Too often, the Christian faith has been discredited by adherents who, in all good faith, have offered facile and sweeping solutions to the world's ills without really understanding the complexities of the situation. More harm than good is done by naïve ecclesiastics who confidently prescribe policies without having adequately consulted the experts in the various fields of human activity. Such ecclesiastics may have good ethical insights, but these are rarely matched by the factual knowledge that is equally necessary to sound moral judgment. In fairness, however, it must also be said that in recent years there has been a good deal of cross-disciplinary work in which Christian ethicists and men with expert knowledge have worked together on such knotty problems as the rights and wrongs of abortion.

It may also be said that in the past few years the problems of Christian ethics have been debated more vigorously than for a long time. There must be few people who have not heard of the "new morality." Certainly, the voices have been confused, and anyone looking to Christian thinkers for guidance on the problems of the day will find himself bewildered. Some clear insights, I believe, have emerged, and we shall take full cognizance of them in what follows. But I am bound to say also that, at least among the more popular presentations of the new morality, too much attention has been paid to the wrong things and too little to the basic problems of theological ethics. For instance, we have heard a great deal about the virtues of "situation ethics," but much of this discussion has been pitiably irrelevant to the major ethical problems of our time.[3]

The present book confines itself to three problems which, I believe, are fairly basic and important, and I shall now say what these are.

1. The first problem is that of the relation of Christian morals to non-Christian morals. By "non-Christian" morals, I

mean, for instance, the morals of adherents of other faiths (Jews, Buddhists, and so on), the morals of humanists and of Marxists, and even—if I may be permitted a somewhat abstract expression—the general moral striving of mankind. Is the relation to be understood in terms of continuity or discontinuity? Is there, to put the question in its most provocative form, really a distinctively Christian ethic at all?

Obviously, there is a sense in which there is a distinctive Christian ethic. Speaking *descriptively,* one can point to the actual historical phenomenon of Christianity with its own literature on the conduct of life, its own patterns and standards of behavior, its own formulations of rules, and so on. These are distinct from, let us say, what we would find in Islam. But when I ask about the relation of Christian morals to non-Christian morals, I am not proposing a phenomenological exercise in comparative ethics. Rather, I am asking whether, underlying the divergent historical phenomena and particular formulations, there are some profound ethical convictions that are held in common.

The question is not only theoretical. It has important practical implications because, in a shrinking world, Christians will find themselves more and more in the position of having to choose whether or not they will cooperate with non-Christians on moral and social issues. Christians realize that they will be living in a pluralistic world. They do not expect that in the foreseeable future all people will become Christians—indeed, it is more likely that Christians will be a dwindling minority in a world in which the expansion of population is taking place mainly among non-Christian peoples. Furthermore, Christians are coming to understand that in the ever more tightly knit world of rapid transport and instant communication, they cannot "go it alone." Already they are finding that they must cooperate with non-Christians to achieve certain goals—perhaps with Buddhists in Asia for the sake of peace, or with humanists in the United States for the betterment of oppressed groups, or even, in some parts of the world, with Marxists for the establishment of a more just economic order.

Other groups are likewise beginning to understand that they can do little on their own and are holding out their hands to Christians. H. J. Blackham, director of the British Humanist Association and author of an outstandingly clear and judicious book on humanism, remarks that "humanists alone cannot hope to bring in the open society" and forecasts that "humanists and Christians and others are going to have to work more closely on the common human tasks and problems."[4]

Parallel to these exchanges between Christians and humanists is the Christian-Marxist dialogue. Admittedly, this dialogue is confined to a very few persons on either side, and it has to make its way against a legacy of very deeply rooted hostility and suspicion. Admittedly, too, some of the Christian contributions have been extraordinarily naïve—they remind me of nothing so much as the conversations my friends and I used to have when we were undergraduates at the University of Glasgow in the years immediately before World War II. Yet the fact that such contacts have been established and that hostility is giving way to mutual respect and the possibility of mutual cooperation is something that will be welcomed by all except the most bigoted.

But are we to say that such instances of cooperation, as between Christians and humanists or, even more, between Christians and Marxists, are to be understood as merely tactical or pragmatic decisions, imposed by the exigencies of special situations? Or are they (as I intend to show) instances of genuine cooperation, having not merely a practical motive but also a theoretical (and theological) foundation, in the sense that there is continuity between Christian morals and what I have called the "general moral striving of mankind"—something which is foundational to the morals of Christians, Marxists, Buddhists, humanists, and others?

It is of course well-known that it has always been part of the Marxist philosophy to make tactical adjustments of policy to meet special situations. For instance, in World War II, Stalin relaxed the persecution of the various religious groups for the sake of promoting national unity in the great patriotic war. But those most deeply involved in the new Christian-Marxist dialogue do not think that this is just a tactical affair, and that they will return to their former hostility once the immediate aim has been achieved. Paul Oestreicher writes: "Undoubtedly there are some who promote the dialogue for tactical reasons. Most do not. They do it because they believe . . . there is a connection between Jesus of Nazareth and Marx the prophet."[5]

Admittedly, some enthusiasts for the dialogue see the connection in terms that are too facile and that ignore profound differences. A major difference, for instance, is the central place which Christianity gives to reconciliation, and the very marginal place accorded to it in Marxism. But if we allow for the necessary qualifications, I believe Oestreicher is correct in claiming a deep-lying connection between Christianity and Marxism, and we shall try to discover what it is that binds together in their moral endeavors men of different faiths and ideologies.

Let me say at the outset, however, that there is one way that we must avoid, and that is the glossing over of genuine differences so that one side tries to annex the other or jumps onto the other's bandwagon. Such procedures can only be inimical to the kind of cooperation that is sought.

Thus, I deplore the annexationist tendency among some Roman Catholic apologists of talking about the good humanist or Marxist as an "anonymous Christian"; or the similar tendency among Protestant exponents of the new morality who tell us that "wherever there is love, there is

Christ." To talk in such ways is to infringe on the integrity of humanists, Marxists, and others who, in many cases, have studied Christianity and consciously rejected it. Instead of trying forcibly to baptize them, we should openly acknowledge that their moral achievements are accomplished within their own frames of reference and are not obscure forms of Christianity. I find myself in agreement with Dietrich Ritschl when he asks: "Is not the idea that reconciliation between a Communist husband and wife, forgiveness between Moslems or love between confessed non-Christians is secretly 'Christian' an indication that the 'new moralists' advocate a most subtle and tastelessly indirect form of Constantinian Christian imperialism? Can they not leave alone the non-Christian fellow-man who tries his best to give love and reconciliation . . . and can they not abstain from conquering him with 'Christian' categories?"[6] Unless we can return an honest affirmative to Ritschl's question, I think the prospects for understanding and moral cooperation between Christian and non-Christian will be dim.

Equally objectionable is the attempt by Christians (or others) to capture for themselves the prestige of another group. Thus, according to Paul Oestreicher, Christians and Communists "both claim to be proponents of genuine humanism."[7] (The expression "genuine humanism" would seem to imply the judgment that there is a lot of false humanism about.) But have Christians and Marxists any right to claim for themselves the title of "genuine humanists"? Admittedly, the expression "humanism" has had several meanings in the course of history, and no one would deny that there are humanistic elements in both Christianity and Marxism. But it is doubtful if either of these movements could qualify as "humanism" in the sense in which the word is currently used by those who avow themselves to be humanists. H. J. Blackham gladly acknowledges the humanist strands in Christianity and Marxism but writes that "the great humanist tradition is not best represented now nor likely to be handed on impressively by either the Communists or the churches."[8] Probably both Christians and Marxists are moving today toward emphasizing the humanist elements latent in their traditions. But they cannot glibly claim to be representing "genuine humanism," and they have a lot to live down. Movements which produced the Spanish Inquisition and the Stalinist purges, the Scopes trial and the Lysenko affair, will need to work hard to change their images if they want to be accepted as supporters of the humanist ideal of the "open society." They are not likely to conciliate so-called "scientific humanists" by claiming for themselves that they are "genuine humanists."

So our first problem is to explore what is common to Christian and non-Christian morals, but to do so in such a way that genuine differences are respected and the integrity of different groups is not impugned.

2. Our second problem is closely related to the first one. What is the shape of a theological ethic appropriate to our time?

I say that this problem is closely related to our first problem, for the shape of a theological ethic will largely depend on whether one considers Christian morals to be continuous with non-Christian morals or discontinuous. Most exponents of the "new morality" have proceeded as if the Christian ethic is discontinuous with all other ethics. They have begun with the notion of love as we find it in the New Testament or with the Christian community as the context of action or with some other distinctively Christian idea. They frequently contrast the New Testament ethic with that of the Old Testament, as an ethic of love as opposed to an ethic of law.

Now, it is clear that there can be no quarrel with an account of Christian ethics that sets out from the teaching of the New Testament. Nevertheless, when one adopts a method which begins with what is *distinctive* in Christian ethics, one is less likely to develop and stress the thought of what is *shared* with other approaches. Thus, in opposition to the prevailing tendency, I think the shape of a theological ethic should be such that we begin by exploring what is common to Christians, Buddhists, Marxists, humanists, and others alike.

There is a parallel here between the methodological problem in Christian ethics and that in systematic theology. I have for long argued that in a secular and pluralistic age, the starting point for systematic theology should be the consideration of the meaning of humanity, rather than the doctrine of God or even the doctrine of Christ.[9] To be sure, I do not suggest that other approaches are incorrect, but I do believe that the anthropological approach has a peculiar appropriateness at the present time. Now the same seems to hold in ethics. Instead of beginning with Christian love or some other distinctive or supposedly distinctive Christian concept, it is appropriate to begin by considering man, and especially those aspects of man which are of special significance for ethics. Such a consideration will, I believe, reveal moral foundations that belong to our humanity as such, irrespective of whether we are Christians, Marxists, Jews, or anything else. Moreover, on the basis of this foundational morality it will be possible for the Christian to appreciate the love, concern, and goodness of many a non-Christian without resorting to the impertinent idea that such a person must somehow be a "hidden Christian."

In saying that an investigation into the being of man forms an appropriate starting point for the exposition of Christian ethics, I am not, of course, proposing anything that is especially novel. Although Protestant ethics (and especially recent ethics influenced by Karl Barth) has tended to found itself on what is distinctive to Christianity, there is a long tradition of moral theology among Catholics,

Anglicans, Lutherans, and others which always has begun with the question of man. The first chapter in a textbook of moral theology has usually been on "man and his end"; that is to say, it has dealt with the common humanity which we all share, irrespective of our religious or ideological convictions, or the lack of such. It seems to me that this method, although it has lately been out of favor with many people, holds great promise for Christian ethical thinking at this time when we have to relate more positively than ever before to the ethical thinking of non-Christians.

Having discussed the nature of man, moral theologians have gone on to consider the principles of conduct which accord with man's nature, that is, to the so-called "natural law." This concept seems to me to be acquiring a fresh importance, and it offers the most likely basis on which to establish secure moral bonds between Christians and non-Christians, such as that "connection between Jesus of Nazareth and Marx the prophet," of which Paul Oestreicher has spoken.

But while the moral theology of the past offers some methodological advantages, its content needs drastic and even revolutionary change and updating. So if we are going to take "man and his end" as the starting point of a contemporary theological ethic, this must not be the Aristotelian man who has survived until lately in the moral theology textbooks, but the "new man" of the technological age, the man who is disclosed to us in contemporary psychology and phenomenology. This is man in the midst of change, so that it has become doubtful whether one can still speak of a human "nature." Likewise, if we are going to try to rethink the meaning of "natural law," we must not think of either human nature or cosmic nature in the static manner that has been customary in traditional moral theology. If it has become questionable whether man has a "nature" in the sense of the fixed essence once attributed to him, and if the cosmos is to be conceived in this age of genetics and nuclear physics and the expanding universe not as a static hierarchy but in evolutionary and dynamic terms—then the whole concept of a natural law becomes very problematical and would certainly need to be radically revised.

Clearly, formidable difficulties lie ahead in the way we have chosen. But it is better that we should face such difficulties than evade them in the manner that has been characteristic of much of the "new morality." In the chapters ahead, we shall devote considerable attention to the question of man, and of a foundational morality which may serve as firm bridge between Christian and non-Christian morals. It will be the "new man" that we have in mind—the man of the modern age, caught up in rapid change. But we may be surprised to find that in many ways he is not so far removed from the "new man" of the New Testament. So we use the expression "new man" with deliberate ambiguity, to suggest both the man of today and the new creation in Christ.

3. The third problem that will occupy us is that of the place of faith in the moral life, the problem known traditionally as that of the relation of religion and morality. This problem arises very acutely as one works through the two problems already mentioned. If, as we have indicated, we are going to argue that Christian moral ideals are fundamentally akin to the ideals of non-Christian morals, and if we are going to hold also that the appropriate way to unfold the Christian ethic is to begin by expounding the nature of the humanity common to Christians and non-Christians alike, then does not Christian faith become superfluous and irrelevant to the problems of ethics? Is it not enough that people should be human and moral, leaving aside their Christianity or their Buddhism or their Marxism or whatever particular religion or ideology has shaped their morals? And would it not indeed be a good thing for this to happen, since it can hardly be denied that religious and ideological

rivalries have from time to time diverted men from the common goals of the moral life, divided them among themselves, and even produced conduct that has been downright inhuman?

Many people would agree with the remark of Ludwig Feuerbach: "Wherever morality is based on theology, wherever the right is made dependent on divine authority, the most immoral, unjust, infamous things can be justified and established."[10] Of course, one may readily substitute in this sentence "ideology" for "theology" and "political" for "divine" and the complaint still stands.

Let me at once concede that the question of morality and religion is a very difficult one. Certainly, in the modern world, morality cannot be based on some arbitrary religious authority.

Furthermore, in any discussion of this problem, we must be very careful to avoid the kind of answer which attacks the integrity of the other side. It is outrageous, for instance, for the religious person to claim (as he sometimes does) that one cannot have morality without religion, as if the person who is devoid of faith cannot take the moral demand with full seriousness; and it is equally outrageous when the secularist claims that the Christian's conduct is moral only because he is motivated by prudential considerations concerning rewards and punishments.

I shall in fact maintain that there is a positive relation between morality and religion, but I shall try to do so without for a moment saying anything that might seem to question the integrity of those who consciously separate morality from any religious connection. I shall argue that Christianity, properly understood as both a theology and a spirituality, provides a context of belief and formation that is supportive of the moral life and its complement. In greater or less degree, I suppose that one might make similar claims for other religious faiths; and perhaps even for nonreligious ideologies which stress moral ideals and teach that there is hope for their realization—though possibly even to say this is to imply that such ideologies are not entirely nonreligious. Undoubtedly, there are forms of humanism which have a definitely religious strand. However, I am not wanting to argue that somewhere we are going to find hidden Christianity or crypto-religion in the serious-minded humanist—I have already criticized such "annexationist" arguments. Let a humanist speak for himself. Blackham tells us: "Not worship, but a total participation in the world is the humanist's aspiration. Humanism is not religion, but it is more than 'morals without religion.' "[11]

But would not these considerations lead us to the belief that the most heroic kind of morality, perhaps even the purest kind of morality, would be that of the man who combined moral devotion with complete irreligion? If there were a man who did not believe in any supportive context for his moral action and who even supposed that the world is absurd and frustrating to human aspirations, yet who nevertheless threw himself into the moral struggle, would we not have to say that this is the highest type of morality and that a morality which relates itself to religious faith is adolescent by comparison? Admittedly, the kind of person we have in mind would be very rare. It is true that one may think of Albert Camus, who visualized man's position to be as hopeless and absurd as that of the mythical Sisyphus, rolling a great stone up a slope over and over again, only to see it crashing back down. Yet Camus saw this godless situation as a challenge to greater moral effort.

However, as Camus himself acknowledged, one can hardly stay indefinitely with a sheer nihilism. Schubert Ogden remarks that "the notion of the absurd hero . . . can hardly define a real possibility."[12] There is something like an inherent contradiction in the notion that everything is meaningless and frustrating, yet morality is worthwhile. But the

2 Problems of the New Morality

Of all the forms of renewal and rethinking that are going on among Christians today, perhaps the most controversial and explosive is the "new morality." People are indeed reluctant to change their beliefs and their ways of worship, but they seem to feel even more threatened if they are asked to change their patterns of behavior, and especially if it is suggested that they should abandon some of their ancient taboos.

It must be acknowledged that there are a few enthusiasts who have presented the new morality in such extreme and sensational ways that the impression has been given that this new morality constitutes an attack on Christian standards and encourages a reversal of traditional values. Every movement for renewal has its lunatic fringe, and since this usually gets much publicity, one can understand something of the alarm which may be generated.

Though we may not be willing to go along with some of the extreme forms in which it has issued, we should be ready at once to acknowledge that a "new morality" or a new moral theology is a vital need for our time, and there is much in current and recent ethical thinking among Christians that must be welcomed. As I have indicated already, the new techniques, knowledge, and powers which multiply with the progress of science and technology bring with them moral problems for which there are no precedents and which demand fresh moral thinking. The demand is reinforced when we consider the new insights which man has gained into his own being from contemporary developments in biology, psychology, and philosophy. But what is perhaps the most compelling reason for seeking a new morality is the simple and universally acknowledged fact that today's sophisticated world does not blindly accept rules that rest on authority and tradition. This does not necessarily imply the rejection of the content of the tradition, but it is the demand for explanation and elucidation and even for intelligent participation in the formulation and revising of rules and standards. The challenge to authority in ethics is only part of a much wider phenomenon, seen also in the challenge to the universities, the family, political institutions, and so on. In every case, there is discontent with an authority externally imposed. This discontent is justifiable. The "new morality" is prepared to face this discontent with the traditional and the authoritative, and to interrogate the Christian ethic about its *rationale* and its foundations. This must lead to a better understanding of what Christian morality is and what concrete demands it lays on us in our time. But, more importantly, it will promote responsible and intelligent conduct among people who see something of the reasons behind Christian morals, rather than supposing that they rest simply on a theological *fiat*.

Actually, when one comes right down to concrete issues, the prescriptions of the new morality are rarely different from those of the old. This is true, for instance, on the much debated question of chastity. No doubt contemporary Christian moralists will advocate chastity on different grounds from the moralists of the last century, and certainly they do not simply appeal to an authoritative rule or to fear and guilt feelings. But this is all to the good, for it means that the contemporary moralist is asking for a more responsible and adult attitude toward sex than, generally speaking, the older moralists did.

No contemporary moralist that I have read advocates promiscuity, but his reason for condemning it is that it is a most irresponsible abuse of the sexual capacity. On the other hand, he will not merely lump together as "fornication" sexual acts outside of marriage without making some discriminations among them, and this too is a responsible approach to the question. If the impression has got abroad that the new morality is exceedingly permissive in matters of sex, the reason may be that some of its advocates have an unfortunate habit of making much out of very exceptional (and frequently fictitious) cases. But when we come back from these to the ordinary cases about which ordinary people have to decide, then the prescription of the new morality is usually the same as that of the old. In fact, readers who go to some much publicized and sensationalized book looking for a "far-out" Christian teaching on sex are frequently disappointed to find that, apart from some extraordinary cases that do present difficult moral dilemmas, much the same patterns of conduct are being prescribed as always have been prescribed.

Strictly speaking, we should not talk of a "new morality" but of a "new ethic," if the term "ethic" is understood here as reflection on morality. This would be an indication that the substance or content of the Christian life remains essentially what it always has been, but that we are being offered a new way of understanding it and of relating it to the problems of today's world. Rather similarly, we talk of "new theology" but not of "new faith." We take it that the substance or content of Christian faith remains, but our thinking about it and our understanding of it change. There is always need both of new theology and of new ethics, if by these expressions we understand new thinking on Christian faith and morals respectively. However, the expression "new morality" seems to have established itself, and since thinking is itself a part of action, possibly new ethical reflection does indeed induce a new style of morality. But I do want to stress that, especially with regard to its prescriptions, the new morality is continuous with the old and that the term "new morality" is misleading if it obscures this continuity.

The expression "new morality" has been used chiefly to refer to the views of certain Protestant and Anglican theologians who have been writing on ethics in recent years, such as John A. T. Robinson, Joseph Fletcher, Paul Lehmann, James A. Pike, and others. One of the most obvious characteristics of this group—though, of course, there are many differences among the people I have named—is that its new ethic is strongly and sometimes even extravagantly in revolt against any supposedly legalistic forms into which the Christian ethic may have been allowed to set. Among Roman Catholic moralists there has been nothing as radical as the "new morality." But the renewal and rethinking that have been going on in the Roman Catholic Church in the past few years have been felt very strongly in the area of moral theology. There is a new emphasis on charity rather than on law, and a new recognition of the place of the individual conscience as against the authority of the church. Bernard Häring has been the leader in this revitalized style of moral theology, and his great work *The Law of Christ*[1] must be accounted a classic in its field. Häring's affinities, however, are not so much with the "new morality" that is being advocated today as with the work of scholars like the Anglican Kenneth Kirk, who a generation ago was seeking to revive moral theology in the Church of England and to adapt the traditional framework so as to give more scope to the free educated consciences of individuals in the modern world.[2]

The New Testament ethic itself first appeared in the form of a protest against a traditional ethic, at least to the extent that this had been allowed to harden into an impersonal system of rules. But it seems to be the fate of every reforming movement to become itself hardened in the course of time, so that new reformations are necessary. We are presently living at a time when a more or less radical renewal and transformation is going on throughout the whole fabric of Christianity, and this renewal must affect ethics just as much as theology or liturgy.

Furthermore, it cannot be denied that Christian morals had been allowed to harden in legalistic ways scarcely compatible with the spirit of the New Testament. This hardening went on among both Protestants and Catholics. In the Puritan tradition and in Catholic moral theology alike, there have been attempts to spell out detailed rules on matters that can hardly be regarded as of first importance —for instance, Puritan regulations concerning Sunday observance and Catholic regulations concerning the eucharistic fast. The overwhelming weight of rules tended to smother the spirit of Christian morals altogether. The new ethic demands more flexibility, more of the open and personal quality that has been characteristic of Christian moral teaching from the time of Jesus himself. It asks that we attend more to the concrete situations of life and less to the generalized laws that sometimes operate in harsh and impersonal ways.

The tension between the new morality and some of the older formulations is often set out in terms of an opposition between situationism and legalism, an ethic of context versus an ethic of law. Alternatively, the opposition is expressed in terms of persons and principles, as in the slogan: "Persons before principles!"; or there may be a simple antithesis of love and law.

But much of the argument that has gone on in such terms has been, in the words of James M. Gustafson, "a misplaced debate."[3] To set up such disjunctions is to oversimplify the problem, and to miss the very complex texture of moral behavior. One is not presented with an "either . . . or. . . ." Christian love and the concrete personal situation are of the greatest importance, but one can also exaggerate this importance. Because of such exaggeration, the "new morality" has cut itself off from saying anything significant about the really urgent moral issues of our time; and it has also cut itself off from any genuine dialogue with the adherents of non-Christian morals. These criticisms, here summarily stated, will be developed more fully in the rest of the chapter.

Let us acknowledge that legalism is assuredly a distortion of Christian morals, and perhaps of any human morals. Undoubtedly there have been legalistic elements in the way Christian morals have been presented. Nevertheless, the legalism attacked by advocates of the new morality seems to me to have been often a straw man. It is difficult to find any thoroughgoing system of legalism, either in the Christian tradition or outside of it. Almost always, ways have been found whereby the rigor of law has been tempered to meet the needs of actual situations. In Catholic moral theology, for instance, an important place has always been given to casuistry, the science and art of applying general rules to particular cases. Furthermore, there are various systems of casuistry, some more rigorous and others less so. Among those systems, the most influential has been probabilism, and this is precisely the system that allows for most flexibility. So the critics of moral theology have paradoxically attacked it both for rigidity (arising from its formulation of rules) and for laxity (arising from probabilist casuistry)!

The Pharisees are represented in the New Testament as infected with a good deal of narrow legalism, and subsequent generations of Christians have held them up as the type of rigorism, and of hypocrisy as well. But modern scholarship has rejected this caricature. No doubt there were bad Pharisees, but most of them were humane and progressive. The New Testament makes it clear that they tempered the rules by considerations of prudence, compassion, and humanity. "Which of you, having an ass or an ox that is fallen into a well, will not immediately pull him out on a sabbath day?"[4]

Even less excusable than the attacks on the Pharisees is the suggestion, found in many books on Christian ethics, that Old Testament ethics were legalistic while Christian ethics marked a new departure of an entirely discontinuous sort, substituting love for law, persons for principles, inward obedience for outward authority. No one who has read Martin Buber will suppose for a moment that Old Testament and Jewish ethics are rigidly legalistic or that the law (strictly, the "instruction" or *torah*) has no regard for persons or is incapable of being inwardly appropriated.

Systems of law have always made provision for the special situation when the hard case arises, and writers on jurisprudence have usually devoted a section to what is called "equity," a word which stands for the spirit of the law rather than its letter. " 'Equity' means natural justice, not simply, but in a special aspect; that is to say, as opposed to the rigor of inflexible rules of law. For the law lays down general principles, taking of necessity no account of special circumstances or individual cases in which such generality may work injustice. In all such cases, in order to avoid injustice, it may be considered needful to go beyond the law, or even contrary to the law, and to administer justice in accordance with the dictates of natural reason."[5] Aristotle recognized something like this principle of equity in his idea of *epieikeia*,[6] and I especially like Matthew Arnold's translation of this Greek word as "sweet reasonableness." My contention then is that even systems of ethics that have made much of laws and rules have had a situational element built into them, so to speak; for they have always been willing to temper their rules in accordance with "natural reason" or "sweet reasonableness."

If it would be hard to find any out-and-out legalists, I think it might be harder still to find any pure situationists. Perhaps there were some in the French resistance movement during World War II, men who recognized no rules at all and whose decisions were determined purely by the situations in which they found themselves. Perhaps there are some existentialist philosophers who (at least in theory) consider that one is in "bad faith" when one conforms one's action to a rule, and believe that, regardless of the requirements of conventional morality, one must in each unique situation decide for the policy in which he will realize his authentic selfhood. But one has to say that the kind of life men lived in the French resistance was quite abnormal, and that the extreme type of existentialist ethic associated with it offers little help for dealing with the moral problems that ordinary people face under more stable circumstances.

I think one would have to say not only that a purely situational ethic must be a very rare phenomenon but that such an ethic, when it is found, suffers from very serious defects. I shall mention several which, taken together, seem to count decisively.

1. No doubt there is a sense in which every act that one performs is unique, but it is also true that it has features in common with other acts. A situational ethic stresses the uniqueness of each act, but its common characteristics are

just as important. In every area of human life there is need for generalization, and the moral life is no exception. Life is too short for innumerable agonizing appraisals undertaken *de novo*. Rules, customs, and habits are not inimical to an authentic human existence, but they save time and effort by capitalizing on experience.

2. More seriously, a situational ethic breaks up the moral life into separate acts in such a way as to deny the reality of a unitary personal self that grows and deepens through its successive experiences. For the situationist, man is simply "functional" man: he is what he does, in one situation after another. But (as I have tried to show in detail elsewhere[7]) true selfhood is attained precisely as one transcends a particular situation and brings it into a unity embracing many situations. Man is more than what he does; out of his acts he builds up the unity of a personal self. Through memory and anticipation he sets up "spans" which encompass many situations, and these spans themselves are embraced in the unity of his total "life-span." The so-called "functional" man, to whom a situational ethic would be most appropriate, would actually be more like a machine than a man. Norbert Wiener, a leading authority on cybernetics, points out that "the machine is intended for many successive runs, either with no reference to each other, or with a minimal limited reference." Because of this, a computing machine is "cleared" between its runs. But man "never even approximately clears out his past records."[8] To put it in a word, man is a person. A person is not arrived at by adding together acts, occasions, and situations; these are, on the contrary, abstractions from the unity of a personal existence.

3. If radical situationism is disruptive of the unity of the personal self, it is even more subversive of any idea of a moral community. One of the most telling objections against situationism is that it is a fundamentally and incurably

individualistic type of ethic. Paul Ramsey is correct in his warning that "no social morality ever was founded, or ever will be founded, upon a situational ethic."[9] And it is because we desperately need a social morality that I felt constrained to write above that the new morality, so far as it has been advocating the virtues of "situation ethics," "has been pitiably irrelevant to the major ethical problems of our time."[10]

4. As well as suffering from individualism, radical situational ethics suffers from the allied vice of subjectivism. The situationist seems to be compelled by his theories to assume an extraordinary degree of moral sensitivity and perceptiveness in those who are expected to read the demands of the situation. Some people presumably do have this intuitive awareness of the right thing to do, but in situations of any complexity at all, especially when there are conflicting demands, most people find themselves perplexed. Few either have or claim to have the moral maturity and the psychological insight that instinctively know the right policy. Most people are likely to be suspicious, and probably rightly so, of the man who claims to follow the "law of the heart." The notion was well criticized by Hegel, who showed that the individualistic "law of the heart" must give way to the universal "law of all hearts," which is by no means impersonal for not being subjective. "The accepted and established laws are defended against the law of a single individual because they are not empty necessity, unconscious and dead, but are spiritual substance and universality, in which those in whom this spiritual substance is realized live as individuals, and are conscious of their own selves. Hence, even when they complain of this ordinance, as if it went contrary to their own inmost law, and maintain in opposition to it the claims of the 'heart,' in point of fact they inwardly cling to it as being their essential nature; and if they

are deprived of this ordinance or put themselves outside the range of its influence, they lose everything."[11]

5. The situationist is less than realistic in the extent to which he is willing to recognize the weakness of human nature and the fact that even our consciences can be distorted. His idealized Christian is always motivated by love. Unfortunately, real people, including Christians, are not like this. There is a place for the prohibiting "Thou shalt not . . ." to keep us from kicking over the traces. Prohibitions can sometimes be stifling, but they can also be protective. They save us from our worst selves.

6. Finally, how does one define a "situation"? Where does one draw the boundaries of any particular situation? Actually, every situation has rough edges and merges into the next one. Furthermore, one can include in it or exclude from it almost as many factors as one may choose. As David Edwards rightly reminds us, "the real situation is likely to be seen as involving more than the emotions of the principal actors in the immediate drama"[12]—though it seems to be with these individual emotions that the new morality is chiefly concerned in its notion of the "situation."

The truth is that the complex texture of morals includes both a rule element and a situation element. The question is not one of opting for rules or situations, law or love, or however it may be expressed, but of trying to do something far more difficult, namely, to strike a right balance or tension between rules and situations. The confusion in much contemporary Christian ethics is due to the fact noted by Thomas C. Oden: "The proper *modus vivendi* between situational ethics and legal principle has not been achieved in our time. The persistent antinomian inclinations of current Protestantism toward an ethic of self-affirmation without self-denial, gospel without law, freedom without obedience, and grace without obligation, constitutes perhaps the most urgent problem of Protestant ethics."[13] Incidentally, Oden suggests that the solution to the problem may lie in bringing the Protestant stress on "Christian liberty" into a fruitful relation with Catholic moral theology, which he describes as "long steeped in an ethic of law and virtue." It is clear that this suggestion is close to my own intention.

It may well be the case that the tension between the situation element and the rule element in ethics will vary at different times in history or in different cultural settings or even in different areas of moral decision. For instance, at times when the bulk of the people is poorly educated, the stress is likely to be on law and there will be a detailed spelling out of rules, whereas in more sophisticated societies more must be left to the enlightened conscience and to the individual judgment in face of the concrete case. Again, a situation ethic has more plausibility in questions of individual behavior than in social questions. Roger Shinn has pointed out that in such an area as sexual conduct, in which individual persons and their unique relations are of great importance, there are strong arguments for allowing weight to the situational element; whereas in such an area as race relations, in which the behavior of groups rather than individuals is concerned, law acquires special importance in regulating conduct and in promoting good attitudes.

Actually, among those Christian writers who advocate the "new morality" we find many evidences of tension between a rule element and a situation element. Even those who claim most loudly to be situationists are not pure situationists, and they bring in rules somewhere or other. Of course, they lay the main emphasis on the unique situation and the demand of love in that situation, and some of them seem to come fairly close to antinomianism. There are, however, many differences among the new ethicists, and we soon learn that some allow more and some less to the situational element.

John A. T. Robinson, formerly Bishop of Woolwich, some-

PROBLEMS OF THE NEW MORALITY | 37

times declares himself very strongly in terms of what appears to be a purely situational ethic. It would be difficult to find in any Christian writer a more thoroughgoing expression of a situational ethic than the following sentence: "Love alone, because, as it were, it has a built-in moral compass, enabling it to 'home' intuitively upon the deepest need of the other, can allow itself to be directed completely by the situation."[14] I draw attention to the phrase: "directed completely by the situation." This seems to render quite superfluous any laws, rules, precedents, or prohibitions.

Incidentally, the sentence quoted also affords a remarkable example of the situationist's utopian belief in his own or other people's sensitivity to complex situations. Is it true that, provided we have love, we can " 'home' intuitively on the deepest need of the other"? On the contrary, what sometimes baffles our deepest love and concern is that with the best will in the world we cannot discover "the deepest need of the other." I suppose that is why we need to have psychiatrists. Human nature has complexities that do not reveal themselves very readily.

Yet in spite of his talk about letting action be "directed completely by the situation," we find Robinson introducing very different considerations. In his ethics, as in his theology, his bark turns out to be more aggressive than his bite, and he usually ends up with a very moderate position. Paul Ramsey's comment gets to the point: "Robinson's voice is the voice of pure act-agapism, but his hands are the hands of rule-agapism."[15]

Ramsey illustrates his comment by quoting another sentence from Robinson, who says: "I would, of course, be the first to agree that there is a whole class of actions—like stealing, lying, killing, committing adultery—which are so fundamentally destructive of human relationships that no difference of century or society can change their character."[16] This certainly looks very much like the introduction of moral prohibitions which hold good no matter the situation. But, in fairness to Robinson, Ramsey ought to have gone on to quote the next sentence, which reads: "But this does not mean, of course, that stealing or lying can in certain circumstances never be right." Robinson is here saying that, in exceptional circumstances, the prohibitions may be set aside. But in this whole passage he seems to have departed very far from that extreme situationism in which we are to be "directed completely by the situation." He seems to be now saying what moralists have always said—that there are rules and prohibitions of very wide application, but there will sometimes be exceptional cases when "sweet reasonableness" will demand that they be set aside.

Incidentally, there are also some semantic confusions here. Words like "stealing" and "lying" already contain moral evaluations, so that one could argue that the sentence "Stealing is always wrong" is a mere tautology. In that case, one should not say that stealing is sometimes right, but rather that there may be occasions when taking someone's property without his consent is not stealing. Linguistic usage is clearer in words which refer to killing. "Murder" is, by definition, always wrong, and if there are occasions on which killing is justifiable, we use a neutral word such as "homicide."

When we turn to Joseph Fletcher, we meet a different type of ethic from Robinson's. Fletcher too is only a qualified situationist, for at the beginning of his book *Situation Ethics*,[17] he makes it clear that his variety of situationism is not the opposite of an ethic of laws but a compromise between such an ethic and antinomianism, the rejection of all law. In admitting this, Fletcher seems to be saying that his ethic is like any other ethic. Presumably he calls it a "situation ethic" because the situational element is stressed much more than the rule element, and as he works out his position, he does in fact seem to come pretty close to anti-nomianism.

Father Häring puts his finger on the essential weakness of Fletcher's ethic when he says that "Fletcher's concept of love is structureless."[18] It is another example of the over-simplified ethic which dwells on the subjective judgment of the agent and his immediate relations to other persons involved in the situation, without having regard to the broader structures of morals and society. "To use love as the great simplifier of ethics," remarks John Bennett, "is to place too much emphasis on the motive of the one who acts and not enough on the sources of illumination concerning what is good for those who are affected by the action."[19]

But if Fletcher's notion of love lacks structure, it does so in a different way from Robinson's. The latter's understanding of love, "homing" intuitively on its target, runs the risk of dissolving into mere sentimentalism, but at least it is a human love with some human warmth. Fletcher's type of love, on the other hand, has a utilitarian and even calculating character. There is an astonishing passage in his book in which he goes so far as to suggest that the decision to drop an atom bomb on Hiroshima can be understood as the result of a calculation in *agape!*[20] The "love" of which Fletcher writes is love without compassion, a calculating impersonal love that is, if I may say so, "as cold as charity." No wonder Bishop Pike was constrained to write that an *agape* which lacks respect for the person, however much it attends to his immediate needs, is not enough and that we need a spot of *eros* as well![21] But Fletcher's understanding of *agape* is not to be taken as definitive or as adequately representing the New Testament's idea of love.

His ethic is blurred further by his constant use of bizarre and often fictional cases, little related to the circumstances of ordinary life. An ethic cannot be built on exceptions. Indeed, hard cases can be recognized only because there is already a tacit acceptance of norms.

Paul Lehmann's ethic is called "contextual" rather than "situational." The two ideas are related, but it has become clear in exchanges between Lehmann and Fletcher that there are important differences. The chief of these seems to be that Lehmann believes that the Christian's policies of action should be determined not just by the immediate situation but by the much wider context of what God is doing in the world.[22] This reminds us of David Edwards' call for expanding our notion of the situation to include the total situation,[23] and undoubtedly Lehmann's contextualism is a great advance beyond the narrow situationism of Fletcher and Robinson. But we are left with the difficult question of how we are to know what God is doing in the world. No doubt we might agree about this in a general way; for instance, Christians believe that God is reconciling the world to himself. But how are we to know what God is doing in some particular situation, or indeed whether he is doing anything at all? Sincere and sensitive Christians may be able to agree in a general way about God's action, but when it comes down to highly particular and complex situations, who has the "hot line" so that he knows God's angle in the affair? The notion of what God is allegedly doing in the world can even be a dangerous one. Anyone who has attended ecclesiastical assemblies knows that bishops and bureaucrats have a marvelous way of sacralizing their own pet schemes by representing them as the politics of God.

Lehmann repeatedly uses in his book an expression which is meant to tell us, in a general way, what God is doing in the world: "making and keeping human life human." We shall return to the consideration of this expression later,[24] and will find it a helpful one, both for developing our own anthropological approach to moral theology and for relating this approach to Lehmann's christocentric one.

In this brief survey of some of the leading exponents of the "new morality," we have criticized the excesses of situationism, though not denying for a moment that there must be a situational element in any worthwhile ethic whatsoever. Excesses apart, has the time come for a new stress on the situational element, as Fletcher and the others declare?

It may well be the case that the complexities of modern society, the unprecedented problems raised by science and technology, and the relative sophistication of many modern people have in fact brought us to such a time, and that the new style of ethics is championing a legitimate interest. On the other hand, we have seen the very definite limits of situationism, especially in the face of the pressing problems of social ethics. Is it then the case (as we have hinted) that the new stress on the situation and its accompanying insights can best be rescued from distortion by bringing them into fruitful contact with some of the insights of traditional moral theology? Perhaps we shall find—as Bishop Robinson has acknowledged—that the old and new moralities are complementary rather than contradictory.[25] Joseph Fletcher, for his part, has remarked that the casuistry of the traditional moral theology makes it more humane and acceptable to the situationist than the simpler but more rigid legalism of Protestant ethics.[26] On the other side, we find Karl Rahner noting that while "radical situation ethics" would be rejected by all Christians, "for Catholic moral theology it cannot cause any difficulty in principle to assert that there are cases of moral decision in which moral theology based on universal essences . . . is not in a position to offer the Christian unmistakable precepts in the concrete case."[27]

The opinions just cited point to a possible development in theological ethics that would take us beyond partial and extravagant positions to a more comprehensive solution. The new emphasis on situations and flexibility does not abolish rules or the task of moral theology, but it does call for a

3   Ethics and the New Man

Who is the man of today? What is his image? How does he understand himself? These questions seem to be scarcely answerable; or, rather, so many answers are proffered that it seems impossible to decide among them.

There are many ways in which the contemporary man understands himself, and there are many images which he projects. We hear of the technological man, the secularized man, the organization man, and so on. We hear optimistic accounts of how man is at last being liberated from poverty, ignorance, and disease so that he can become more fully human; and we hear pessimistic accounts of how the very processes that raise his standards of living may also bring about alienation, dehumanization, and even destruction. Man is hailed as a unique being, the measure of all things, destined to subdue the world. He is also compared to machines, and sometimes the comparison is unfavorable, for there are machines nowadays which can perform intricate mental operations far more efficiently and swiftly than the brain of man. We still hear naturalistic theories of man, representing him as essentially an animal under a thin veneer of culture. The witty and satirical book *The Naked Ape*, by Desmond Morris, is doubtless exaggerated, yet it does burst the bubble of pretentiousness by showing us that much human behavior does lend plausibility to the view that man is at bottom an unusually cunning, aggressive, and lustful primate. And there are still theological accounts of man which see him as the bearer of the image of God, *imago Dei*.

Theories which concentrate exclusively on man's animality or his spirituality or something else are certainly one-sided. Yet all the many theories and images of man that circulate today probably do reflect characteristics really to be found in the immensely complex phenomenon of humanity.[1] To compare, discuss, and criticize these theories would require a book in itself and is obviously a task that cannot be undertaken here. But, in any case, how does one evaluate a theory of man? Such a theory is not like a description of an independent objective reality. The theory itself is a part of man and helps to shape the very phenomenon which it sets out to describe. For instance, if people understand themselves and others as essentially naked apes, this particular image affects their behavior and their relationships. Within limits, man is what he thinks he is.

It is significant that we ask "Who is man?" rather than "What is man?" We ask "What is a star?" or "What is an oak?" or "What is granite?" and these "what" questions are answered by giving an objective description of the "nature" of a star or of an oak or of granite. Certainly, one can also speak of the "nature" of man, but man is more than a nature. Because he understands himself and projects an image of himself, he becomes responsible for who he is. As Abraham Heschel has expressed it, "In asking about man, we ask of man what he knows about himself as a human being. This self-knowledge is part of his being."[2] So if we ask who is the man of today, we look for the answer in the way he understands himself.

In asking about the man of today, we are already implying in our question that he may not be the same as the man of yesterday. There can be no doubt that man's understanding of himself does change in the course of history; and since this self-understanding is itself an important constituent of the human existent, then to say that self-understanding changes implies that the existent, man himself, changes too.

So we have to look for the new man among the images which he currently proliferates. But I have already said that we cannot proceed to a detailed examination of the multitude of theories and images that are to be found today. Our procedure will be more modest, but also, perhaps, more directly related to our purpose. It seems to me that among these many theories and images there are certain common characteristics that keep on appearing across ideological lines. We find them recurring in what the Marxist, the existentialist, and the evolutionist are saying about man, as well as in current Christian thinking about man. Since it is our aim to find a kind of basic common morality uniting Christians and non-Christians and to look for the roots of this in our shared humanity, then these recurring characteristics in the various images of man must be of the greatest interest to us.

Most of the remainder of this chapter will be devoted to exploring five characteristics that seem to pervade the contemporary images of man and spread across religious and ideological lines. I do not suppose that this list of five is exhaustive, but I do think it is rather basic. In each case, I think there is a contrast between the "new man" having these characteristics in his self-understanding and the man of the past, especially Western man in the past few centuries; but we shall also find that this "new man" of the twentieth century has links with the "new man" of whom St. Paul spoke on the basis of Christian and biblical faith. As our exploration of the man of today proceeds, we shall also become aware of its implications for a Christian ethic that will be relevant to the problems of the contemporary world and able to relate to non-Christians who are struggling with the same problems.

1. *Changing Man—a Being-on-the-way*

Perhaps the most striking characteristic of the contemporary man's self-understanding is his recognition that human nature changes. Man is a being-on-the-way. I use this expression to indicate that in his very being, man is on the move. He is always moving on to new images and ideals of himself and to new ways of understanding himself. He is always taking to himself new powers and devising new ways of realizing his projects. Thus there seem to be two ways in which the changes in man take place—one of them primarily inward, intellectual, and spiritual, whereby formative images and ideals are created and projected, and the other primarily physical, consisting in the techniques and apparatus whereby man carries out his operations. Clearly, however, the two ways are very closely related.

We have already touched on the first of these ways in the paragraphs which introduced this chapter. Man not only is, he also has an image of himself; and whenever man adopts a new image of himself, there is a sense in which he becomes a new man, for the image is part of his being. Every new image, concept, or theory by which man reflects on his own being has its effects on his being. "Unlike a theory of things which seeks merely to know its subject, a theory of man shapes and affects its subject. . . . We not only describe the 'nature' of man, we fashion it. We become what we think of ourselves."[3]

The second way in which man changes has to do with his physical constitution. Henri Bergson pointed out that a major difference between man and the animals is that whereas ants, for instance, perform their operations by using parts of their bodies which have become highly efficient instruments for special tasks, man has a relatively unspecialized body and performs his operations by using tools which are not themselves parts of his body. Thus the ant, however efficient, is limited to certain tasks by the very structure of its body; while man, perhaps inefficient to begin with, has infinite possibilities of development. His type of instrument "lays open to activity an unlimited field into which it is driven further and further, and made more and more free."[4]

Now, these tools or instruments which man multiplies become parts of his nature. In Marshall McLuhan's phrase, they are "extensions of man."[5] There is nothing "unnatural" about them, for man's very "nature" is such that he has this kind of adaptability. He is not structurally riveted to some few operations but has a "natural" capacity for an unlimited number of activities. Jet transport, for instance, can now be said to have become part of the nature of man. It is natural for man to travel from New York to San Francisco in five hours; it would be most unnatural to get out the covered wagon and spend weeks on the journey. Television has likewise become a part of our nature—it is natural for us now to see events in Delhi or Rio de Janeiro or even on the moon on the same day that they happen, or often almost instantly. Equally natural, though perhaps more controversial, is the contraceptive pill. Given that human nature is not static but, by its very biological basis, must develop itself by way of "extensions," the pill is just as natural a method of birth control as is the so-called "rhythm" method. But the pill shows us in a very striking way the mutability of human nature. The two functions of sexuality and reproduction, hitherto united in human life, have now become separable. Surely this is an important change in human "nature," and one that raises serious moral questions. No defense of chastity (and, of course, I think it can be defended) can afford to overlook this change, which renders obsolete some of the old arguments for continence.

I have said that the inward and outward changes in man are related. They react on each other. As man develops his instruments, some of them will eventually give him greater control over himself. Recent years have seen great advances in the science of genetics. Men have come a long way toward understanding the physical basis which is determinative even for some of our mental characteristics. Incidentally, we have also learned that there are almost infinite possibilities in the variety of human beings that may be brought into existence. A time will almost certainly come when our knowledge and techniques will have been developed to the point where it will be possible for us to choose what kind of individual is to be brought into existence, even with respect to his inner dispositions and personal qualities. Does this mean then that finally the inward transformation of human nature will be subjugated to the outward and physical modes of transformation? By no means, because precisely if one had the power to determine, through applied genetics, the character of a human person, then one would have to fall back on one's own image of man. There is a reciprocity between the inward and the outward factors that make for change in human nature. In the long run it may be the inward factor, the image or ideal, that will have the say in determining outward factors. But it has to be acknowledged too that in this complex process of change every outward factor—be it television, cybernation, contraception, or something else—has its influence in shaping the inward image.

If I have established that contemporary man understands himself as a being-on-the-way, and that he is in fact caught up in change, I have next to show that this way of understanding man cuts across religious and ideological lines.

Possibly the existentialists have been most insistent in teaching that man is on the move. The very use of the word "ex-sistence" implies this. To "ex-sist" is to go out from any given state in which one finds oneself. Existence precedes essence. Man does not have a static nature, in the sense of a fixed stock of essential properties. A mineral, let us say, does have such a stock of properties, but man is rather a being of possibilities, and he makes his essence or his nature as he decides among these possibilities. Some existentialist philosophers would deny that man has a nature, but it seems to me there are no compelling reasons for dropping the familiar expression "human nature," provided one recognizes that this is not fixed for all time.

However, the attempt to conceive man's being in more dynamic ways than was customary in the past is by no means confined to existentialism. Evolutionary philosophies, in their many forms, are agreed in conceiving man in terms of action, change, and fluidity, and they take cognizance also of his setting in a cosmos which is itself on the move.

Traditional Marxism, to the extent that it was allied to nineteenth-century materialism, tended to be deterministic in its view of man, though it was not quite consistent on this point. But today there are many Marxists who have become disillusioned with Marxist fundamentalism, so to speak, and among some of them the notion of man's transcending himself and fashioning for himself a new nature has become very influential. Charles West sees in contemporary Marxism a movement "in the direction of a philosophy of the continuing self-transformation of man by his activity, both practical and theoretical, in a concrete social situation."[6] These words seem to me to express very clearly the understanding of man as a being-on-the-way which we have discussed above.

Thomism too has moved toward a more dynamic understanding of the being of man. I refer especially to the
"transcendental" Thomism of Lonergan, Coreth, Rahner,
and others. In this view, human nature is "open" so that
man has the possibility of passing beyond himself. The
importance of this understanding of man will become more
evident when we discuss the relative weight of anthropology and christology in Christian ethics.[7]

I have mentioned these various forms of contemporary
philosophy to show that there is indeed something like a
consensus in the understanding of man as a being-on-the-
way. We can never at any moment pin man down, so to
speak, and say: "Here is human nature!" In that very
moment, he is already on his way to something else.

We can assert that this dynamic view of man is very
much in accord with biblical teaching. In the biblical
picture of man there is an openness in his nature. Indeed,
if we are to speak of his "nature" at all, we would need to
say that man's very nature is to transcend himself. We see
man in the Bible as the distinctive creature to whom God
has given the possibility of going out beyond himself into
ever new ventures of faith. This is the creature who is
adopted as a son, and before whom is set a future of
promise and hope beyond what can be imagined. "We are
God's children now; it does not yet appear what we shall
be."[8]

These words remind us that to acknowledge that man is
a being-on-the-way, a being who transcends himself, is
also to admit a mystery in man, if by "mystery" we understand an inexhaustible depth. It is true, of course, that the
word "transcendence" is nowadays used by atheistic philosophers, both existentialist and Marxist (Sartre and
Garaudy are examples), who would strongly deny that it
has anything to do with God or that man transcends toward
God. Yet Heidegger seems to be correct when he claims

that "the idea of transcendence—that man is something that reaches beyond himself—is rooted in Christian dogmatics."[9] At the very least, one can say that the introduction of the notion of transcendence and therefore of mystery into contemporary atheistic theories of man has narrowed the gap between these and the Christian doctrine of man. Marxist participants in Christian-Marxist dialogue have been especially interested in pursuing Christian insights into man that go beyond the merely economic theories of man with which classical Marxism was preoccupied. Czech Marxist philosopher Milan Mahovec has remarked: "No Marxist known to me ever asked to have a chapter of *Das Kapital* read to him on his deathbed."[10]

However, this whole notion of man on the move, man the self-transcending, a being-on-the-way, in spite of the fact that it has some biblical roots, contrasts sharply with the understanding of man that has prevailed throughout much of Western history. Human nature has been considered as something fundamentally unchanging. Traditional moral theology itself thought of man as constituted by a fixed, static essence, in the midst of a fixed and static cosmos. Much was made of the notion of a "natural law" based upon this nature and therefore itself regarded as fixed, static, and even immutable. But if we allow that man's own nature is self-transcending, and if we suppose further that the cosmos is no static hierarchy but an open, evolving, and emerging process of nature, then a drastic reconception of natural law is demanded. I say a drastic reconception rather than the simple abolition of natural law theory. I believe indeed that the concept of natural law has abiding importance for Christian ethics and for non-Christian ethics as well, and that its rehabilitation is an urgent task today. The problem will be considered in a later part of this book.[11] For the present, it is enough to say that the natural law can be rehabilitated only if it too is set in motion. There must be a flexibility about natural law and a built-in principle of development, so that as man learns more of his own nature and as he extends his control over the nature that lies about him, he gains new insights into the order in which he is placed and experiences its obligations in new ways.

Does the acknowledgment that human nature changes and its implicate that there is no unchanging natural law mean that we are plunged into a thoroughgoing ethical relativism? I do not think that this is the case. There are some constants which maintain themselves in the flux. To abandon static ideas of man and nature for more dynamic ones does not mean that notions of order and structure have been thrown away or that every culture and society, still less, every individual, is made sole author and arbiter of moral values.

A dynamic nature, as I understand it, whether we are considering the nature of man or of the physical world, is not a chaotic and amorphous flux but an existence (or procession) with an order and direction. We have talked of changing man, but we should be clear that there is no virtue in change itself. Change is ambiguous, and may be either for the better or for the worse. Furthermore, to the extent that man is taking over control of himself and nature, there no longer operates some unconscious law of evolution or universal progress, for changes become dependent on human decisions and so, in turn, on the values and images which influence these decisions. There is, I believe, a constant direction implicit in the notion of a dynamically conceived morality, and this makes it different from any sheer relativism or subjectivism. The direction may be defined formally as the direction which leads to a fuller humanity. But clearly this formal expression will need to be given more content.

The demands and obligations imposed on the moral agent

within the context of nature conceived dynamically (whether human nature or universal nature) may not be so easily formulated as perhaps they could be in the context of a nature that was conceived in static terms, but the obligations are no less real and may well prove to be more exacting. They reflect a different historical situation and different, more complex levels of human knowledge and experience.

2. Embodied Man—a Being-in-the-World

The next point that comes up for consideration is that the contemporary man understands himself as a being-in-the-world. The phrase "being-in-the-world" is commonly used among existentialists and phenomenologists to describe the basic condition of the human existent. Their use of this expression implies the assertion that there can be no self without a world with which the self is in interaction. We do not begin with a self to which a world gets added on, so to speak; we begin with the unity of being-in-the-world, and out of this prior unity self and world emerge in a reciprocal relation.

To say that there can be no self without a world is also to assert that there can be no self without a body, for it is in virtue of the body that we are in the world. Only as embodied selves can we act on the world or be acted upon by the world. The body is not an appendage to the self, still less an encumbrance to the self, but an essential part of personal being. The contemporary philosophical understanding of the body is once more largely due to the work of phenomenologists and existentialists, such as Sartre, Marcel, and Merleau-Ponty. I call this a "philosophical" understanding, because it is not concerned with physiological questions about how the body works but with the body as the condition for our participation in a world and for our attainment of personal being—a condition so essential that, as these philosophers point out, it is as correct to say man *is* a body as that he *has* a body. But their essential insights were already anticipated by Feuerbach when he wrote: "The body alone is that negativing, limiting, concentrating, circumscribing force, without which no personality is conceivable. Take away from thy personality its body, and thou takest away that which holds it together. The body is the basis, the subject of personality."[12]

In claiming that the understanding of man as a being-in-the-world, and therefore as a psychosomatic unity, is part of the contemporary image of man, I question whether this particular characteristic of the current self-understanding has as yet achieved the same degree of clarity or can point to the same consensus as the understanding of man as a being-on-the-way. But I believe that it is gradually replacing both the idealist (or spiritualistic) and materialist conceptions of man.

The new view of man, however, has a hard battle to fight to get recognition, for the idealist view of the self has been entrenched for centuries in Western thought, both philosophical and popular. (The materialist view of the self as an epiphenomenon is simply an offshoot of the idealist view, formed in conscious opposition to it and sharing the same basic presuppositions.)

The tradition which I broadly describe as the "idealist" or "spiritualistic" view of the self goes back to Plato, and, beyond him, to the Orphic mysteries. This view emphasized the spiritual and intellectual side of man's being, to the disparagement of the bodily and worldly side. The soul and its inner life were what really mattered. The soul was taken to be the real self and the body its habitation, hardly an integral part of the real person. The tradition has been immensely influential in Western man's self-understanding. It passed on into modern philosophy with Descartes, and until very recently, when it began to show signs of decay, the idealist tradition continued to regard man as primarily the knowing subject while, in varying degrees, the world and the whole spatiotemporal process were supposed to be infected with unreality.

The Christian ethic was early influenced by an otherworldly understanding of man. Certainly, Christians always opposed such extreme positions as Gnosticism, in which man was thought of as an exile or captive in an alien or even demonic world, so that his main aspiration was to escape from it. Yet some Christians have come very near to such a view. In any case, even before the full brunt of Hellenistic influences began to be felt, the eschatological convictions of the earliest Christians encouraged indifference and contempt toward the present transitory age.

In spite of this, it can surely be said that the new emphasis on man as a being-in-the-world is in very close agreement with much of the biblical teaching on man and the world. Admittedly, the most obvious support comes from the Old Testament (and it is noticeable that some of the advocates of a "secular Christianity" are preoccupied with the Old Testament writings), but the New Testament, even with its strong eschatological coloring, is by no means negative to the understanding of man's involvement with the material world.

The understanding of man as a being-in-the-world is implicit in the biblical doctrine of creation. The dust of the ground was just as essential an element in the constitution of Adam as was the breath of life, by which he became a "living soul."[13] He was placed in the garden to tend and care for it, and also to enjoy its produce. The creation story portrays human life as a being-in-the-world, and this is taken to be the work of God, the intention of creation, and therefore good. However, not only the creation story but the whole tenor of the Old Testament, including its ethical teaching, accepts and rejoices in man's being-in-the-world.

This understanding gets its confirmation in the New Testament above all from the doctrine of the incarnation. The very life of God, so Christian faith declares, has entered the world and become flesh. And even if the church from the beginning was influenced by other ideas that could lead to the despising of the world and of man's bodily life, the doctrine of the incarnation prevented these ideas from ever becoming fully victorious. In the first centuries of the church's existence, there was no lack of movements which prized only the spiritual side of man's nature and regarded the physical as inherently evil, the creation of demonic powers rather than of God. But such movements—Gnosticism in its various forms, Manichaeism, and the rest—were denounced by the church as heresies, for they threatened the very *raison d'être* of the church through their denial of any genuine incarnation. Mention must be made also of the doctrine of a resurrection of the body, in contradistinction to theories about the immortality of the soul.

Thus, as far as its fundamental doctrines are concerned, Christianity is well equipped to offer men guidance about their lives in this world. Yet no one would deny that, in fact, Christianity has retained an otherworldly bias, and this has been just as apparent in the puritanism of some Protestant sects as in ascetic movements within Catholicism. But if man is a being-in-the-world, then the notion of a "fuller humanity," which we noted earlier as a formal idea, begins to acquire some content. There cannot be a fuller humanity without a care for bodily existence and an affirmative relation to the world.

This does mean some rethinking of the Christian ethic, a rethinking that is likely to lead it closer to some of the non-Christian ethics of our time. If we take seriously that man is a being-in-the-world, then the Christian ethic, as we conceive it today and as we are likely to conceive it in the foreseeable future, will be less ascetic than it has often been in the past. Not withdrawal and renunciation, but rather right use and enjoyment, should characterize the Christian's attitude to this world in which his existence is set. In Dietrich Bonhoeffer's way of putting it, we have to be concerned with the penultimate or next to last things before we come to the ultimate or last things.[14]

There is a striking expression in the papal encyclical *Progressio populorum*. Pope Paul VI declares there that man must *know* something and *have* something before he can *be* something. The Pope is in effect saying that "being" and "having" are not always in opposition to each other, as Christians have sometimes seemed to suggest. On the contrary, there is a basic level of having that must be attained if one is really to be human. There is, so to speak, a floor of material well-being through which people must not fall if they are to live with the dignity and decency appropriate to humanity. Such mundane matters as food, health, housing, education, and the like cannot be extrinsic to Christian moral concern, as if we needed only to concentrate on some rare and exalted virtues of the inner life. There must be concern for man's whole life as being-in-the-world. The Christian Church has, of course, from time to time in its history caught glimpses of these wider implications of its moral commitment, but today the whole matter has become one of the greatest urgency. This is not primarily because contemporary man understands himself as a being-in-the-world or because some Christians are reflecting anew on the doctrines of creation and incarnation, but above all because of the pressures of an almost eschatological world-situation—a situation in which technology enables the production of wealth to go forward at ever increasing speed while, simultaneously and paradoxically, the human race becomes more and more deeply divided as vast millions fall below that level of *having* which is essential to the dignity of *being* human.

While I have said that the Christian ethic of today will be less ascetic than in the past and less ready to suspect that sin must be lurking somewhere in any enjoyment of the gifts of creation, this does not imply that the ethic will be more lax or that the time has come to encourage an indiscriminate pursuit of affluence and self-indulgence. If there is a floor of having below which it is hard or impossible to be fully human, I wonder if there may not also be a ceiling of having above which a genuinely human existence becomes very difficult. "It is easier for a camel to go through the eye of a needle than for a rich man to enter the kingdom of God."[15] If there is a poverty that dehumanizes, there is also an affluence or acquisitiveness that dehumanizes, though in a different manner. Man must have something in order to be something; but there is no simple correlation between the extent of his having and the depth of his being.

I pointed out near the beginning of this discussion of embodied man that the understanding of man as being-in-the-world or as a psychosomatic unity has rendered obsolete not only the spiritualistic, otherworldly understanding of man but also the opposite and equally one-sided understanding of man, the materialistic. This has to be borne in mind in any attempts to rethink the Christian ethic in relation to the world, for the materialistic view of man leads to forms of ethics that are quite incompatible with Christianity. Among these forms are the sensualism and paganism which are so strongly condemned by the biblical writers, from the Hebrew prophets to St. Paul. By "sensualism" and "paganism," I mean the kind of attitudes which make the satisfaction of bodily needs the highest good for man. This pagan kind of immersion in the world is certainly widespread today and in the affluent lands is sedulously propagated through the many channels of advertising. We must be careful that it does not infect the Christian quest for a more affirmative attitude toward the world and the body. Allan Galloway has justly

warned: "At a time when the notion of secular Christianity
is rightly receiving a good deal of distinguished attention,
it is of the utmost importance that it be clearly understood
that there is a secular paganism as well."[16]

As against this danger, we must note that to call man a
"*being*-in-the-world" is to recognize that he is not just part
of the world but that, alone among all the finite beings that
we know, he has a measure of transcendence of the world
and that he loses his distinctive humanity when he gets
simply absorbed into the world. To put the matter in a
different way, alongside the truth of man's being-in-the-
world must be set the other truth of his being-on-the-way,
the truth of his transcendence and ex-sistence.

These points are clearly recognized in Bonhoeffer's distinction of the penultimate and the ultimate, and in Pope
Paul's recognition that men must have in order to be. There
is an order in these ideas which the pagan philosophy re-
verses. This pagan (or sensualist) philosophy makes the
penultimate into the ultimate and teaches that we *are* in
order that we may *have*. It is the manifestation of what
Christian moralists have long known as concupiscence
(*concupiscentia*), a kind of insatiable desiring. This distorted kind of desire is well characterized by Paul Ricoeur:
"It is the infinity of desire itself, taking possession of knowing, of willing, of doing, of being."[17] It turns everything
around and subordinates the higher to the lower. It does
not fulfill man but dehumanizes him and continually increases his desires; and, to quote Ricoeur again, "the punishment for desire is desire itself."

As against this sensualist or pagan attitude to the world,
a Christian ethic that accepts man's being-in-the-world also
accepts the subtle dialectic of this far from simple mode of
existence. Thus, if it must eschew the otherworldliness which
has often distorted it in the past, it must continue to eschew,
as it always has done, the pagan pursuit of the multiplication

of possessions and enjoyments as ends in themselves. Man cannot find himself along that way.

But the trouble is that a dialectical understanding is always difficult. One has only to look at the history of Christian thought to find how often one-sided ideas have seized the minds of theologians, usually as hasty correctives to equally one-sided aberrations which they were meant to correct. The "new morality" and "secular Christianity" have both not been lacking in overreactions which could be fatal to their legitimate goals. We must not allow the intoxication of release from puritanism and otherworldliness to swing us over into undialectical and uncritical world-affirmation. This could be the way to a neopaganism just as oppressive to man and as diminishing of his humanity as the paganisms of the past.

But, exaggerations apart, we acknowledge being-in-the-world as one of the characteristics of contemporary man's self-understanding, and one which must be taken into account when we try to give content to the idea of a full humanity. A renewed Christian ethic must pay more attention to man's worldly and bodily character than it has done in the past if it is to be able to meet the needs and challenges posed by the age of affluence and technology and if it is to be open to cooperation with concerned non-Christians. To work out the details of such an ethic will be a difficult and laborious task, involving specialists from many disciplines, but the theological guidelines are emerging clearly enough.

3. *Social Man—a Being-with-Others*

The next characteristic of the contemporary self-understanding calling for attention is that man is a being-with-others, essentially social or communal in his being. Just as there can be no self without a world, so there can be no self apart from other selves. It is not the case that, first of all, I exist, and then I take note of other selves and relate myself to them, as if this relation to others were something extra that gets added on to a self which is already there. Rather, the relation to other selves is necessary to constitute me a self. In the language made famous by Martin Buber (though he was not the first to have this insight), the "I" is constituted through the "Thou"; or, alternatively, the words "I" and "Thou" have meaning only as already contained in the primary compound word "I-Thou."[18] Community belongs to the very being of man.

The discovery or rediscovery of our fundamental being-with-others is, like our being-in-the-world, an idea that is having to fight hard for acceptance because it is so much in conflict with the understanding of man that has been dominant in some earlier generations. I think it would be fair to say that the Renaissance, the Enlightenment, and the nineteenth century were all periods when Western man understood himself in a predominantly individualistic way. There is an interesting illustration of this in the thought of three representative figures from these periods—Thomas Hobbes, Jean-Jacques Rousseau, and Sigmund Freud. Whatever the differences among these men, they all held forms of the so-called "social contract" theory. Presumably none of them believed that this theory gives an actual historical account of the origins of society, but what is significant about the theory is its supposition that the individual is the basic reality, the unit or building block, so to speak; and that society is subsequent to the individual and is formed by adding together individuals who have already a measure of completeness in themselves. As against this, a modern phenomenology of man (and empirical studies seem to reach similar results) thinks of the individual as emerging from a prior social whole.

Acceptance of the idea of man as a being-with-others is

another factor that demands a rethinking of the Christian ethic and that will open channels of communication with some non-Christian ethics. There can be little doubt that the individualism of Western man in the past few centuries was strongly influential in determining the way in which the Christian life and ethic were understood by different types of believers. Catholic pseudo-mysticism and Protestant pietism have alike been concerned with the quest for individual salvation, though it seems to me that if one gives the matter a thought, the idea of "individual salvation" is really a contradiction in terms. How can anyone be saved or made whole without the neighbor and the community of which he is part? Again, the Christian virtues have been understood almost entirely in terms of those personal qualities that make for individual integrity. There are in many of our cities stately Victorian churches reared by the piety of prosperous manufacturers who, in many cases, seem to have been unaware of any discrepancy between a strict personal integrity in private life and the oppressive character of their public policies in the operation of an economic and industrial system that had little compassion toward the laboring classes.

It is true that a good deal of individualism lingers on, and we see its philosophical expression in some forms of existentialism. But, on the whole, Christians seem to be getting beyond individualism. The liturgical movement and the new sense of social obligation are evidences of this.

But apart altogether from what philosophers and theologians may be saying, the unfolding of history itself seems to be bringing the age of individualism to a close. We are being compelled to abandon it, as all our lives become more closely entwined together and as our interdependence increases. As people live more and more closely together in urban and suburban societies, and as swifter and swifter communication and transportation bring all the parts of our planet into a tightly knit whole, both individuals and nations have to recognize that their destinies are bound up with the destiny of the whole. Marshall McLuhan seems to be right in saying that what is commonly called the population *ex*plosion is better understood as a population *im*plosion in which we are all being thrown together. Whether we like it or not, the fact of our being-with-others presses inexorably upon us.

Some people, of course, do not like it. This fact reminds us that mere physical togetherness is a long way from an authentic being-with-others, which introduces existential and ethical dimensions as well as the physical proximity. Everyone knows the paradox of city life; people are tightly packed together, but often there is no communication, only tragic loneliness and indifference. Then there are all the barriers that we erect to prevent being-with-others. Middle-class citizens flee from American cities to all-white suburbs to avoid being-with-others, where the others are of a different race. But millions of black citizens cannot be kept forever at arm's length, and they keep pressing on. The sensible thing would be to accept them as neighbors now. Some Western politicians have worked hard to keep China out of the United Nations. But the vast millions of Chinese are on the doorstep, and they must eventually find their place in the community of nations. The longer we are in finding a *modus vivendi*, the more dangerous the situation will become. As the domestic problems of the United States become more severe, there is emerging a new breed of isolationists who want America to avoid overseas commitments and to concentrate on bulding the affluent society at home. But in the kind of world in which we live, the richest and most powerful nation on earth cannot escape worldwide responsibilities and the expenditure of resources which they demand.

All these forms of segregationism, individualism, and

isolationism are trying to go against the stream of history, and they cannot succeed. Sooner or later, we all have to face our being-with-others, and at the present rate of implosion it had better be sooner.

If the contemporary phenomenological analysis of man is stressing that he is essentially a being-with-others, and if the conditions of our historical epoch are pushing us toward the recognition of this social dimension of our being, it may also be claimed that such an understanding of man is thoroughly biblical, even if Christianity has in fact frequently lapsed into individualism. Recalling once more the creation story, we note that sexuality is basic to the human constitution. Adam was incomplete without Eve. She was created to be "a helper fit for him"[19]—and this expression makes clear that the sexual relation is much more than a physiological one. It is a true being-with-another. To illustrate the parallel between the biblical and the contemporary view, I will again quote Feuerbach, who, in a remarkable way, anticipated such later writers on these matters as Berdyaev and Buber. He wrote: "The distinction of sex is not superficial, or limited to certain parts of the body; it is an essential one. . . . Hence personality is nothing without distinction of sex; personality is essentially distinguished into masculine and feminine. Where there is no 'Thou,' there is no 'I'; but the distinction between 'I' and 'Thou,' the fundamental condition of all personality, of all consciousness, is only real, living, ardent, when felt as the distinction between man and woman."[20]

This high claim for sex as the paradigm of the "I-Thou" relation is essentially biblical, though it has been overshadowed in the church's history by negative attitudes toward sex. Yet it is this high claim which, more than anything else, provides a firm basis for the practice of chastity; for if sex is not just another physiological function but pervades man's personal being as the fundamental capacity for

his being-with-another as an "I" with a "Thou," then merely
casual or promiscuous relations are seen to be destructive of
what is essentially a personal and human relationship.

But sex is only the beginning of the biblical recognition
of man's basic sociality. The history with which the Bible
deals is the history of communities rather than of individuals. There is first the community of Israel and then the
new community of the church. Moreover, both of these communities, in the vision of their most perceptive representatives, were understood not as closed privileged groups but
as, in some sense, foci for all mankind. The overarching conception of New Testament ethics is the kingdom of God, and
the kingdom potentially embraces all mankind. The uni-
versalist spirit and outlook of Christianity was well understood by such early fathers as St. Irenaeus, but the vision
was later obscured by the quest for individual salvation
(which, as I have already suggested, is a self-contradictory
idea) and by the rise of unfortunate misinterpretations of
the notions of election and predestination.

Today it is imperative that Christian ethical thinking not
merely recover but develop in ways hitherto unprecedented
the social and, indeed, international or global outreach of
Christian morals. It is no longer enough to seek personal
integrity and the domestic virtues. There must be concern
with the large structures of human society and with such
overwhelming problems as those of economic justice and
international relations. Of course, it is above all in such areas
that Christians will have to work along with others.

Even today, when one talks about the Christian life or
the Christian virtues, one thinks mainly in terms of individual qualities. But perhaps it would help us to move into
the new style of thinking required of us if we concentrated
our attention on an obviously social virtue, such as peace,
rather than laying the stress on love, as has customarily
been done. Peace is the most inclusive of Christian virtues,

not, indeed, opposed to love, but rather love writ large, so to speak. The Hebrew *shalom*, "peace," a word signifying something much more affirmative than the mere absence of strife, already foreshadows the nature of this inclusive virtue, for the root meaning is something like "wholeness" or "totality." This notion transcends any private or personal virtue (and also rules out any notion of individual salvation) by pointing to the fullness of authentic human existence *in a community*. The Hebrew ideal of peace is further developed in the New Testament. When Jesus says, "Blessed are the peacemakers; for they shall be called the children of God,"[21] he is surely implying that to seek the wholeness of authentic human community is to participate in God's own creative work. A Christian ethic for our time alive to the need for authentic being-with-others may profitably devote much more attention than has been given in the past to the exploration of this great biblical idea of peace and the ways to its realization. Furthermore, it seems clear that this particular biblical and Christian virtue is one which effectively lends itself to the establishment of affirmative relations between the moral aspirations of Christians and those of other religious and humanistic groups. How much more fruitful this approach might be than attempts to show that *agape* or something else is quite distinctive and unknown outside of Christian faith!

But we must notice that the task implied in working out an ethic that takes fuller cognizance of man as a being-with-others is once more a dialectical one, just as we have seen in our discussion of being-in-the-world. If a contemporary Christian ethic must turn away from the individualism of the past, it must not be stampeded into an equally defective collectivism. It is here that possibly Christian-Marxist dialogue could be very helpful. If Christians in the past have had the fault of individualism, Marxists have suffered from the fault of collectivism. Both groups have become dissatisfied with their former stances, and both need to move on to a new concept of community that would transcend the individualism of the one and the collectivism of the other. A true being-with-others, an authentic *shalom,* preserves the personal dignity, freedom, and integrity of the individual within a healthy social structure. The Christian ethic remains as much opposed as it always has been to all forms of oppressive collectivism, whether of the left or of the right.

This has to be said because there are enthusiasts in the church today who disparage personal integrity and domestic virtue as merely "bourgeois" or "tribal" morality and suggest that all that is required is the manipulation of social structures. This is another instance of the kind of oversimplification that is so easy in ethics. The Christian is faced with the more demanding task of trying to work out an ethic that allows for the fullest development of the individual within an equitable social framework. Both personal and social virtues are essential to a full humanity. To pursue the one without the other is a caricature of Christian morals. The moral health of a society is not finally separable from the moral condition of its members.

4. *Man as Agent*

Our next point is that the contemporary man thinks of himself primarily as agent, one who acts and gets things done rather than one who merely thinks about his world. Modern Western philosophy was strongly influenced for a long time by Descartes' famous argument: I think, therefore I am. This has been called the strongest argument in philosophy. But more recently it has come under fire from all sides. A generation ago, William Temple was already calling this argument the Cartesian *faux pas,* the false step that had set Western philosophy on the wrong track: "If I were asked what was the most disastrous moment in the history of

Europe, I should be strongly tempted to answer that it was that period of leisure when René Descartes, having no claims to meet, remained for a whole day 'shut up in a stove.' "[22] But Temple has been followed by a host of others who tell us that we must go back and find a less abstract starting point for philosophy than pure thought. Thought does not go on in a vacuum or, normally, "shut up in a stove." Thought is an abstraction from the wider concrete reality of man's action in the world.

One of the most persuasive statements of the new position is given by British philosopher John Macmurray. He talks of the "primacy of the practical" and proposes "that we should substitute the 'I do' for the 'I think' as our starting-point and center of reference; and do our thinking from the standpoint of action."[23] This sentence is important also as showing that Macmurray, while stressing action, retains the importance of thinking in the context of action. Action is quite different from mindless activism, and we shall have to bear this in mind in our discussion.

Macmurray is by no means alone in stressing the primacy of the practical. Existentialists and pragmatists are with him. Marxism has always made the point—one recalls especially Marx's eleventh thesis against Feuerbach, often quoted: "The philosophers have only *interpreted* the world in various ways; the point, however, is to *change* it."[24] Certainly, in the twentieth century, man has been more and more engaged in changing the world, in acting upon it, and we may expect this to increase. Marshall McLuhan sees television as a powerful factor inducing our participation in what goes on in the world, and events seem to bear this out.

Throughout much of its history, and in some of its greatest representatives, such as St. Augustine and St. Thomas, Christianity has rated the intellectual virtues above the practical virtues. But if we go back to the biblical sources, it cannot be doubted that the intellectual activities of man are understood there as related to the concreteness of life. Of knowledge as it is understood in the Bible, Rudolf Bultmann writes that it is "more than appropriated information; it must realize itself in suitable action." This knowledge involves the whole person. It is "perception accompanied by emotion or, rather, by a movement of the will, so that lack of knowledge is an offence as well as a mistake."[25] The thinking or knowing of the Bible is therefore not of the abstract speculative variety which only interprets the world. It is the thinking of an agent who acts on the world.

Action implies freedom, and with the introduction of this word we strike on one of the most essential of all human characteristics, yet also one of the hardest to define. Freedom belongs to the transcendence and mystery of the human person. Freedom, of course, has often been denied in favor of determinism, sometimes by theologians, sometimes by materialists. But even if freedom has been denied in theory, it has been assumed in practice, otherwise we would never urge anyone to adopt a particular policy and we would never blame anyone for not adopting such a policy. Today especially there is a great demand for freedom—a demand that makes sense only on the supposition that man has a say in shaping his own history and destiny.

The free action differs from a mere happening, such as a snowfall, because the action has an inner side to it, in virtue of its freedom. The action flows from a human choice. In action, as Hegel expressed it, we let the "inner" get outside of ourselves, so that it becomes transformed into something "other" and becomes a constituent of the world.[26] There is in action an awesome creativity. Through his free action, man releases forces which shape the world and society.

As everyone knows, action itself is ambiguous. We can help our neighbors or injure them; we can use the resources of nature or abuse them; we can beautify the world or we can ravage and pollute it. And because there is a risk in all action, since we cannot see all the results that will flow from our action, we sometimes effect evil when we mean to do good; and we took note at the beginning of this book that precisely one of the difficulties of our complex modern world is this ambiguity whereby what we intend for good may turn out to have unexpected deleterious side effects.[27]

But whatever the ambiguity of human action, my purpose at the moment is simply to assert that the capacity for free action is essential to being a man, and that where freedom to act is denied, there is a diminution of humanity. Dignity is taken away, and man's capacity for creativity is destroyed. We quoted earlier the encyclical of Pope Paul VI in which he says that man must *know* something and *have* something in order to *be* something. I think I would like to add that he must *do* something to *be* something. He must have the power to act, for without that power he does not share in the creativity of humanity, nor does he participate in shaping the world by letting what is "inner" to him be released as a constituent of history. The "black power" phase of the history of the American Negro is a good illustration of the point. James H. Cone writes: "Black power means black freedom, black self-determination, wherein black people no longer regard themselves as without human dignity, but as men, human beings with the ability to carve out their own destinies."[28] Surely this is an entirely just demand. It is never enough that something should be done *for* people. If they are to have human dignity, they must have the power to act for themselves. They must have their share in shaping the world and society.

In this connection, I have insisted elsewhere that the essence of love is "letting-be."[29] It is an imperfect love that only cares for the other or does something for him, and it can easily become mere possessiveness. Creative love is precisely the love that makes creative—the love that enables the other to act for himself and to achieve himself.

The Christian ethic then, as we understand it today, must take the risk of increasing freedom and power among those who have been deprived of them. It is true that freedom itself is ambiguous, and it must be expected that some will abuse it. But it is an even more important truth that there can be no full humanity without the freedom to act and to exercise the creative capacity. If the notion of man as agent points to the concreteness of human existence in all its dimensions, as distinct from various abstract ideas of man, then this notion, like those we have already considered, helps to furnish content to the formal notion of a "fuller humanity," which we have taken to be the goal of the moral life.

But, as in our discussion of other characteristics of the contemporary man's self-understanding, we must end this one on man as agent with a warning against distortion. To understand man as agent is quite a different notion from that of "functional" man—the view that man is simply what he does. The notion of man as agent is the outcome of a protest against the abstractness of man as subject; but functional man, as Gabriel Marcel has so well shown, is a new abstraction. Equally abstract and mistaken is the disjunction sometimes set up between doing and thinking, and the anti-intellectualist bias that goes with it. As we have insisted earlier, action is not mere activity; it has its inner side, and it includes thinking as a necessary constituent of anything worthy to be called action. Concerning one of the greatest philosophers of action of the last hundred years, Maurice Blondel, a commentator writes: "If there is anything that repels him, it is to have recourse to any kind of irrationalism or blind voluntarism."[30] The wholeness of man's being is not exhausted by his functions. He is more than what he does. Out of what he does he builds up the mysteries of selfhood, personhood, community.

5. *Man Come of Age: Responsibility*

Nowadays we often hear the expression "man come of age." It implies that he has passed through a period of tutelage and has come to adulthood. At first sight, the notion of man as a being-come-of-age may seem to stand in contradiction to the notion of man as a being-on-the-way, and we are asserting that both notions belong to the contemporary self-understanding. However, I think that they are compatible. Although I have said that man is a being-on-the-way and so always unfinished, I think one may also say that there have been some fairly definite stages on the way; and that currently man has reached a stage on the way where he has taken over a considerable measure of responsibility both for himself and for his world. This is what I want to indicate by the expression "man come of age," though I use it with considerable reluctance because it has been made something of a slogan in recent theology.

It is, in fact, a very imprecise expression and—like the similar expression, the "new man"—seems to be commonly used in two quite distinct senses, a secular one and a biblical one. It is used to point to the condition of contemporary man in the age of science and technology. This man has to a considerable extent discarded the mythological mentality; more and more he has taken the world and the conditions of human life under his control, and consequently he is less and less dependent for his well-being on forces outside of himself, whether natural or supposedly supernatural. The other sense in which the expression "come of age" is used is the biblical one, most fully expounded by St. Paul and given new attention in recent years through the writings of Gogarten, Bonhoeffer, and the "secular" theologians. According to the apostle, every Christian has come of age.[31] Christ has delivered his followers from subservience to worldly powers, and among these is the domination of the law. The law was appropriate during the time of man's minority, so to speak, but now he has passed from its tutelage, and it is open to him to become an heir with Christ and a son of God, and to enjoy the liberty of the Christian man.

These two senses of the expression "man come of age" provide another link between Christian and secular ethics. The important ethical notion associated with this idea of having come to maturity is responsibility. Actually, this notion is receiving considerable attention in current Christian thinking. Responsibility, or, perhaps better, responsiveness (*Verantwortung*), is a major concept in the great work of Bernard Häring, mentioned earlier,[32] in which the moral life of the Christian is seen as a response to the call of Christ. Among Protestant writers, Fritz Buri is the one who has perhaps most decisively built his theology of the Christian life on the notion of responsibility. "God," he claims, "is the mythological expression for the unconditionedness of personal responsibility."[33] Both Häring and Buri freely acknowledge man's responsibility. He is "come of age" in the sense that he must freely decide and is not a child on whom some authoritative moral code can be externally imposed. Yet both of these theologians are also claiming that responsibility means an answerability in the face of a transcendence which lays an unconditioned claim on the human conscience—a transcendence that men have called "God." This is perhaps the place where it becomes most difficult to relate Christian and secular ethics, and we shall give the matter closer attention in the later chapters of this book. Meanwhile, let me quote further from Buri: "Without mythological discourse about the voice which calls us to responsibility, we cannot achieve clarity concerning the essence of the unconditionedness of responsibility. It goes without saying that this voice addresses us in our language, arises in our hearts, speaks to us from out of our surroundings; and yet, it is not merely the voice of my heart, my neighbor, my situation. In the objectivity of our inner and outer world, there is no unconditionedness, but only demonstrable relativity. To be sure, we must not overlook this relativity of our objective world because it serves for the proper enactment of the unconditionedness of our personhood. But in the midst of these relativities occurs the voice, without the awareness of which we do not achieve personhood."[34]

This concept of responsibility has a peculiar relevance to the situation of our time, when man has, to some degree, "come of age." Children, presumably, need detailed rules, and these must at first be externally imposed by an authority. But in adult life, while indeed we still need some basic principles, we have to apply these in concrete situations on our own responsibility. There was a time when the church tried to legislate for most of the situations in which its members might be expected to find themselves. Sometimes the rules were particularized in such minute detail as to be quite ridiculous. That kind of moral theology has surely now been left behind as no longer appropriate to a relatively sophisticated age. In the enormously complex world of today, more and more must be left to conscience and responsible judgment. In medicine, politics, economics, and many other matters, only the experts in such areas fully understand all the factors that are involved, and one has to trust their responsible judgments. This does not mean that it has all become a matter of technique. It means rather that each one has to become his own moral theologian or his own moral philosopher. There are, after all, two kinds of knowledge required for a responsible moral decision—knowledge of moral principles and knowledge of the factual circumstances of the situation. In an increasingly specialized world, only experts in the various fields have the second kind of knowledge. This implies that Christian morality will become increasingly a lay morality.

These developments, which arise from the contemporary Christian ethicist's recognition of man's coming of age and his responsibility, are to be welcomed and help to bridge the gap with secular ethics. But the Christian moralist, holding that double sense of "man come of age" which we have noted above, does not interpret responsibility as meaning that man has now taken all power into his own hands and exercises it in complete autonomy. Man has not become the measure of all things, and his adult freedom, as the Christian understands it, is not to be confused with that subjective will to power which has been a major drive in the recent history of Western civilization and has sometimes manifested itself in demonic forms.

There is, I think, good reason for following Häring and Buri in relating responsibility to a transcendent reality befor which man stands under judgment. In Christian terms, this reality is God, and theologically the freedom and power of modern technological man has to be understood in analogy with the freedom and power of Christian man. In admitting man, his own creature, to a free and adult share in the shaping of the world, God has by no means placed the world at man's absolute disposal or given it over to his unlimited exploitation. Admittedly, some of the "new" Christian moralists talk as if this were the case. They are fond of quoting the verse in which God commands Adam to subdue the earth and have dominion over the creatures.[35] (Incidentally, they always leave out the first part of the verse, "Be fruitful and multiply," which is somewhat less appropriate to our current situation!) But what they forget is that there is another side to responsibility.

A warning comes out of that moving book by Ulrich Simon, *A Theology of Auschwitz*. Man, according to Simon, "is made to be like God, but never to be God. The doctrine of the divine superman died at Auschwitz, and with it anthropology as a disguise for theology."[36]

The distinction between being like God and being God is an important one. Man's destiny is certainly to be like God, and technology will continue to place in man's hands more and more godlike powers. Man cannot shrink from these, nor should he. But he can handle them with responsibility only if he resolves to be like God without being God. Unfortunately, the decades after Auschwitz have shown that the doctrine of the divine superman did not die there, and there may have to be many more occasions of atonement before it dies.

Will it die only if we attain to the kind of responsibility of which Christian moralists write—a responsibility which acknowledges man's adulthood as a being-come-of-age but which also claims that he is answerable to a moral order that he has not himself created? Yet, if we say this, are we not finally separating Christian morals from secular morals, and undoing that bond which seemed to have formed between them insofar as Christian theologians have been stressing the other, liberating aspect of responsibility?

I do not think that we are separating the two. When the idea of responsibility is explored, even in terms of a secular ethic, we seem to enter that area of man's being in which we strike against something of his mystery and transcendence, to use terms which nonreligious writers also employ. For where does one find the limits of responsibility? I am responsible to myself. Also, I am responsible to my neighbors and to the various social groupings to which I belong. But then one must go further and expand this responsibility in time. I am responsible to people in the past, whose heritage I have received. More important still, I am responsible to future generations—and we are only just beginning to appreciate the overwhelming weight of this responsibility, as we grapple with problems of air and water pollution, the significance of ecology, and the wasteful exploitation of earth's resources. As the space age develops, we understand that our responsibilities may be further enlarged. Is it unreasonable to speak, even in secular terms, of our "cosmic responsibility"? But this is at least a considerable step toward the Christian notion of a responsibility before God, for, at bottom, this means that we recognize that we have a small part in the total venture of creation. We are not the measure of all things, but the co-operators in something larger than we understand. The Christian thinks of himself as the steward of creation rather than its absolute lord; and it is interesting that in Paul's remarks on Christian liberty and adulthood, the man who is free is precisely the man who can say, "Abba, Father."[37]

Roger Shinn makes a useful distinction between what he calls "closed humanism" and "open humanism." In "closed humanism," man is indeed the judge of all: "the nonhuman world is the field of conquest; its only value is its value for man." As against this, "an open humanism sees man in his wider setting."[38] I do not believe that the Christian view of man has the possibility of being reconciled with a "closed" humanism, but I see considerable kinship between it and an "open" humanism. In saying this, I am not trying to annex the open humanist as some kind of crypto-Christian—I have already indicated that I think this kind of apologetic is contemptible. But I believe that Christians and humanists (including some Marxists) may well come closer together as they understand their own humanity better. The Christian on his side is abandoning some of the more naïve and mythological ways in which he has thought of God; the humanist on his side is acknowledging a transcendence and a mystery in man that were denied by old-fashioned naturalism. The meeting ground between the two lines of thought could be an expanded and deepened notion of responsibility.

In this chapter we have looked at some basic characteristics of the contemporary man's self-understanding, and we have tried to link these both to the biblical understanding of man and to various secular images of man. We have also been inquiring about the implications for Christian ethics, for the new self-understanding is bound to bring new priorities and new shifts of interest and energy in the moral life.

But before we conclude the chapter, we have to ask the question about the *end* of this contemporary man, for we were proposing to follow the traditional order of moral theology, which customarily began by asking the question of "man's last end." By "end" we mean, of course, the goal of human existence, not its termination, even if the more threatening aspects of the atomic age have made this other meaning a more realistic possibility than it has ever been before.

But can we properly talk of an "end" of man, in the sense of a goal toward which he moves, if we accept the dynamic view of human existence set forth earlier in this chapter? This question seems to me rather like the one which asks whether there is a human nature. Man has neither an end nor a nature in the sense of some fixed, invariable, uniform condition in which he either is now at rest or will come in the future to be at rest. His end, like his nature, is open, and perhaps every end attained opens on the vision of a new one. But if we bear in mind this dynamic character of man's end or goal, there is no reason for not using the expression. The end of man is not something extrinsic to himself. It is fuller humanity, and the discussions of man in this chapter have begun to supply some content for this formal expression.

The traditional Christian view of man's end represented

it as the vision of God. Man, it was claimed, would find his self-fulfillment and his deepest bliss in the attaining of this vision. The moral value (or disvalue) of an action was to be measured by the extent to which it either helped (or hindered) the attainment of the end.

It must be acknowledged that this talk of the vision of God as man's last end or ultimate goal seems—at least, on first glance—to be remote from the analysis of contemporary man carried out in the preceding pages. It seems to take us back to all the things that we have seen contemporary man turning away from—otherworldliness, individual salvation, abstract intellectualism, a state of rest rather than a constant going out from oneself. However, it may be the case that if the expression "vision of God" conveys such ideas to us, then we are fundamentally mistaking its meaning; and that, just as we have to rethink the shape of a Christian ethic, in the light both of the biblical sources and of contemporary man's self-understanding, so we have to rethink the meaning of the vision of God.

Perhaps the simplest answer to the question about man's end is to say: "Man's end is *to be!*" He attains his end when he *is*, in the fullest manner that is open to him. In this sense, his end need not be regarded as coming *at the end*, but can be present in the midst of his life. As we have spelled it out above, man really *is* (that is to say, really attains his end) when he ventures forward in hope, as one on his way and not bound to an unchanged and unchangeable order; when he accepts his life in this world and lays hold on the rich possibilities that it offers; when he acknowledges his being-with-others and joins with them in building a community of concern and love; when he enlarges his freedom of action; when he exercises his power in responsibility.

Here I have used secular or nonreligious language to describe man's end. Yet I have also indicated that when one explores the depth of meaning in such words as "responsi-

bility" or "self-transcendence" (words now freely used about
man by secular writers, including some Marxists) one has
to look beyond man to the wider setting of human existence.
I would wish to claim that to be, really and fully, in all the
dimensions of his existence, man must respond to a reality
that transcends his own. In the first instance, this may be
the reality of the neighbor or the community; beyond that,
it may be the reality of history; and can we stop short
finally of recognizing a responsibility in the face of that all-
embracing Reality that founds all others, the Reality which
religion calls "God"? For man to be in the fullest sense (I
would claim) he must be responsive to "the power not
ourselves making for righteousness," to use Matthew Arnold's
splendid expression for the mystery of God.

But when we describe man's end as to be, and then try to
fill out the details and implications, we begin to see that
this contemporary way of conceiving man's end may not be,
in principle, so very different from the traditional belief that
man's last end is the vision of God, "the Love that moves the
sun and the other stars."[39] We are indeed denying that man's
end is a quietist, individualistic, otherworldly absorption,
which would be a kind of death in any case; but we are
asserting that it is nevertheless a vision of God—an existential vision gained through responsible participation in all the
dimensions of existence in which we find ourselves, including those dimensions that we can only call "cosmic" and
"transcendent."

I should say also that while I have dwelt on the end and
the vision that are possible for man in the midst of his life in
the world, I by no means deny the possibility of an eschatological consummation in which the knowledge of God and
the vision of God will be raised to a new level. This has always been part of the Christian hope, and while sympathiz-
ing with the new emphasis on the secular in Christian ethics,
I have tried not to oversimplify the matter and to maintain

a true dialectic. I heartily agree with Sten Stenson's perceptive comment: "The contemporary rush of Christian theologians to . . . 'this-worldly' theology is a valuable corrective of a centuries-long isolation of religion from common life in some quarters of Christianity, but we must not suppose for that reason (as some radical theologians seem to do) that all 'other-worldly' and 'churchy' stereotypes are therefore a threat to the renascence of viable Christianity. There obviously are many ways of responding symbolically (intelligently) to reality in its relation to human existence. And each way is both a vision and a hindrance to vision."[40] I would indeed affirm that the phenomenology of man as the self-transcending being points toward a destiny that cannot be conceived in this-worldly terms. This style of argument is not, of course, new, but it has recently been receiving attention again as one of the strongest strands in the new theology of resurrection associated with Pannenberg[41] and others.

However, I do not propose here to become involved in eschatological speculation. In a book dealing with ethics, we are concerned with our conduct here and now and with the ends that shape this conduct. The end of man of primary concern to ethics is the vision of God that we can have in this world through our responsible action in it.

4 Rethinking Natural Law

In the last chapter we reviewed some of the characteristics which seem to be pervasive contemporary images of man and which recur in different philosophies and ideologies. We found also that the characteristics discussed are compatible with the biblical understanding of man, and even implicit in it. To take them more seriously would lead to new emphases and new priorities in a contemporary statement of Christian ethics, and these new emphases would in turn strengthen the links between Christian morals and what I have sometimes called the "general moral striving of mankind," as this manifests itself in humanism, Judaism, Marxism, and various other non-Christian life styles.

We must now explore further the common ground between Christian and non-Christian morals; and in doing this, we shall at the same time be advancing our consideration of another question announced at the beginning of the book, the question of whether, at least under present circumstances, the most appropriate way of doing Christian ethics is the way that sets out from the nature of man, rather than ways that begin from distinctively Christian concepts.

The next step after our discussion of contemporary human nature is to consider the notion of natural law. A recent important symposium, *Christian Ethics and Contemporary Philosophy*, ended with a thoughtful essay by the editor, the Bishop of Durham, on the theme: "Toward a Rehabilitation of Natural Law."[1] Although my own approach will differ from the Bishop's, I agree with him about the need for a rehabilitation of natural law, or, at least, for the recovery of what was of abiding value in the notion of such a law. Indeed, I believe that a viable account of natural law could make a vital contribution toward the three major problems from which we set out—the linking of Christian and non-Christian morals, the shape of a contemporary Christian ethic, and the relation between faith and morals.

But natural law—like the corresponding natural theology —is in bad repute nowadays. For a long time it has been under fire from many Protestant moralists, who prefer a christocentric approach. More recently, even some Roman Catholic moral theologians have begun to doubt whether in their tradition too much stress has been laid on natural law and too little on the New Testament. Much of the criticism of natural law has been justified. Any attempt to reformulate it in a better way will be neither an easy nor a popular undertaking. But I believe that such an attempt is urgently required.

A good starting point for our discussion is the assertion, often heard nowadays among theologians who are interested in the relation of Christianity to the secular world, that to be a Christian is simply to be a man. Presumably the expression is an echo of Bonhoeffer: "To be a Christian does not mean to be religious in a particular way, to cultivate some particular form of asceticism (as a sinner, a penitent or a saint) but to be a man."[2] "To be a Christian is to be a man"—what does this mean? Certainly, this statement when made without qualification can be misleading, and it often is. It can be understood as diluting Christianity to the point where it loses all identity; and it can also be understood in the objectionable sense of "annexing" all men to Christianity. Yet, although it can be misunderstood and oversimplified, the statement is, I believe, true in a fundamental way. So far as Christianity offers fulfillment or salvation, it offers a full humanity—or, at least, a fuller humanity.

An illustration of something like this point of view is to be found in the work of Paul Lehmann. We have already noted that, in his view of Christian ethics, the policies of the believer should be determined by "what God is doing in the world."[3] If we ask, "Well, what is God supposed to be doing in the world?" Lehmann repeatedly gives this answer: "Making and keeping human life human!" Obviously, this expression is not intended to be a mere tautology, and therefore we must assume that the word "human" is being used in a different (though related) sense on each of its two occurrences. It is in fact fairly clear that God is said to be making and keeping human life "truly human" or "authentically human" or "fully human"; and that there is therefore implied in this assertion a criterion by which a truly human or fully human life may be recognized.

Lehmann does indeed tell us what his standard of such a true humanity is—it is the "mature manhood" of the New Testament, to be tested by being set against the "measure of the stature of the fullness of Christ."[4] The "fullness of Christ" therefore is, for Lehmann, the criterion of the fullness of humanity, and so—although at first sight his idea that the business of Christian morals is to join in the work of making human life authentically human might seem to provide a liberal formula for relating the Christian ethic to general moral principles—he offers a strictly christocentric definition of authentic humanity. Furthermore, he has very few good things to say about secular moral philosophy.

However, I do not think that one must take up a christocentric position. Even if the Christian ethicist holds (as presumably he does) that authentic humanity is to be judged by the standard of Jesus Christ, there is a kind of reciprocity involved in this assertion, so that one might also say that Jesus is recognized as the Christ because he has brought to fulfillment the deepest moral aspirations of mankind. There is a hermeneutic circle here: Christ interprets for the Christian the meaning of authentic humanity or mature manhood, but he is acknowledged as the Christ or the paradigm of humanity because men have interpreted him as such in the light of an idea of authentic humanity that they already bring to him and that they have derived from their own participation in human existence. No doubt the Christian finds that his idea of authentic humanity is enlarged, corrected, and perhaps even revolutionized by the concrete humanity of Christ, yet unless he had some such idea, it is hard to see how Christ could ever become Christ for him.

At this point we may profitably turn to some of the current trends in christology. Among all theological schools there is widespread agreement in placing a new emphasis on the humanity of Christ. The attempt is made to think through from his humanity to his deity, thus following a route opposite to the traditional one, which speculated on how the divine Logos became flesh.

Two examples will provide an illustration of what we have in mind. In the background of them is an understanding of man as a being-on-his-way, similar to the idea which was sketched out in the preceding chapter. Thus Karl Rahner has argued that, from one point of view, christology can be considered as a kind of transcendent anthropology. Christhood is seen as the fulfillment of humanity, the manifestation of what a true humanity ought to be. "Only someone who forgets that the essence of man . . . is to be unbounded . . . can suppose that it is impossible for there to be a man who, precisely by being man in the fullest sense (which we never attain), is God's existence into the world."[5] Our second example is the christological study which David Jenkins undertook in his Bampton Lectures.[6] He begins by inquiring about the meaning of human personhood, and he goes on to interpret Christ as the "glory of man," a phrase suggesting a humanity brought to such a level that it becomes transparent to deity. Of course, neither Rahner nor Jenkins intends to reduce christology to anthropology. Jenkins explicitly says: "The reduction of theology to anthropology was the prelude to reducing anthropology to absurdity."[7] But both of these theologians do believe that a contemporary christology may well take its departure from what we know of the concerns and aspirations of men and show how these reach a fulfillment in Christ; and if human existence has in it the transcendence and mystery which we have seen reason to believe it has, then such a procedure will not fail to do justice to the transcendent dimension of christology. Even the "death of God" theologians recognized in Christ a kind of ultimacy which, if fully analyzed, would go beyond any "merely" anthropological view.

To put the matter in another way, Christ does not contradict but he fulfills our humanity; or, better expressed, he both contradicts it and fulfills it—he contradicts our actual condition but fulfills what we have already recognized deep within us as true human personhood.

These christological considerations are obviously of the highest relevance to our task of trying to relate Christian ethics to the moral aspirations of people who are not Christians. One can agree with Paul Lehmann that the moral criterion for the Christian is Jesus Christ; but if Jesus is recognized by Christians as the Christ because they acknowledge him, in Rahner's phrase, as "man in the fullest sense" or, in Jenkins' way of putting it, as the "glory of man," then the distinctively Christian criterion coincides with the criterion which, even if only implicitly, is already guiding the deepest moral aspirations of all men—the idea, however obscure, of an authentic or full humanity. In traditional theological language, this implicit image toward which man tends in transcending every given state of himself is the *imago Dei*.

In what sense, however, can the Christian believe that Christ does in fact fulfill the potentialities of man, so that his christhood can be considered as a kind of self-transcending humanity which is also the very image of God?[8] What kind of "fullness" or "perfection" can be attributed to him, so that he may be taken as the criterion of "mature manhood"? Of course, it must frankly be acknowledged that there are some humanists and others who find Christ much less than a paradigm for mankind. Yet even today it is remarkable how many non-Christians join with believers in acknowledging the stature of Christ. The usual complaint against Christians is not that they take Christ as the measure of human existence, but that they fail so miserably to do so! But why does the Christian make the claim he does for Christ, in his humanity?

It is quite obvious that Christ was not perfect in the sense of fulfilling all the potentialities of humanity—indeed, the very notion of this kind of perfection would seem to be self-contradictory, for no finite person could realize in himself within a limited life-span all the possibilities of human life. As far as we know, Christ was not a great painter or a great husband or a great philosopher or statesman. One of the most human of all activities is decision. Everyone, in the limited time at his disposal, has to make choices, to take up one vocation rather than another, to marry or to remain single, and so on. To decide (Latin: *de-cidere*, to cut away) is precisely a cutting away of some possibilities for the sake of the one that is chosen. Decision is to be understood as much in terms of what is cut away as in terms of what is chosen. In a finite existence, self-fulfillment is inseparable from self-denial.

Perhaps when we talk of the "fullness" of Christ, we have to look for it in this very matter of decision, so that the fullness is, paradoxically, also a self-emptying, a renunciation of other possibilities for the sake of that which has the greatest claim. We recall the parable of the merchant "who, on finding one pearl of great value, went and sold all that he had and bought it."[9] Can we say that Christ's fullness or perfection is attributed to him because he gave up all other possibilities for the sake of the most distinctively human possibility of all, and the one that has most claim upon all men, namely, self-giving love? And can we also say that because this love is the most creative thing in human life (for it brings men to freedom and personhood), then Christ manifests the "glory of man" by becoming transparent to the ultimate creative self-giving source of all, to God? And if indeed Christ is understood as the revelation of God, then this surely strengthens the argument for a basic affinity between Christian and non-Christian morals, for what is revealed or made clear in Christ is also implicit in the whole creation. In saying this, I am not "annexing" the whole creation to Christ but rather claiming that what is already present in the whole creation is gathered up in Christ. In other words, I am trying to link Christian and non-Christian moral striving not on the ground of a doctrine of redemption but on the ground of a doctrine of creation.

Christianity, I wish to assert, is not a separate moral system, and its goals and values are not fundamentally different from those that all moral striving has in view. Yet it cannot be denied that there are some ways in which the Christian ethic differs from non-Christian ethics. It seems to me that the differences have to do with the different ways in which the several groups or traditions perceive the goals that are implicit in all moral striving, and the means to these goals; or with the different ways in which they understand and engage in the moral obligations laid upon all; or with the different degrees of explicitness to which the idea of an authentic humanity has emerged in the several traditions.

Of course, there are often differences of prescription between Christian and non-Christian morals. For instance, Christianity prescribes monogamy, while some other traditions do not. But the question of judging between these prescriptions would be settled by still deeper moral convictions shared by the two or more traditions, namely, by asking which prescription best protects and enhances the true humanity of the persons concerned. A distinctive ethical tradition may help its adherents to perceive some aspects of the general moral drive with a special clarity, though equally it may dull their perception of other aspects. For instance, it could be argued that in developing its marriage institutions, the Christian tradition has been more perceptive of what makes for a true humanity than has the Islamic tradition; but one could claim on the other side that Islam has shown itself more perceptive than Christianity in fostering good racial attitudes that put human dignity before color or ethnic background. But fundamental to both traditions is respect for the human person and the desire to enhance human well-being, and this is the implied standard in any comparison of their actual prescriptions and institutions.

We are saying then that what is distinctive in the Christian ethic is not its ultimate goals or its fundamental principles, for these are shared with all serious-minded people in whatever tradition they stand. The distinctive element is the special context within which the moral life is perceived. This special context includes the normative place assigned to Jesus Christ and his teaching—not, indeed, as a paradigm for external imitation, but rather as the criterion and inspiration for a style of life. The context further includes the moral teaching of the Bible, and the ways in which this has been developed and interpreted by the great Christian moralists. There are also the practices of prayer and worship, which are formative for the community and its members. And, not least, there are the many ways in which the moral life is influenced (and, as I hope to show, supported) by Christian faith and hope.

Can we now try to spell out more definitely the nature of that common core which, as I have claimed, underlies and relates all the several moral traditions of mankind? Here we must return to the theme to which a brief allusion was made earlier—to natural law. I said that this proposal would not be very popular in some quarters, and yet, when we inquire why some Christian ethicists object so strongly to the idea of natural law, we find that they give very strange reasons. They seem to be afraid that to allow any weight to natural law would somehow infringe on the uniqueness of the Christian ethic. They seem to be afflicted with an anxiety that Christianity must somehow be distinct and perhaps even have some kind of monopoly of moral wisdom.

For instance, Paul Ramsey in one of his early books asked the question: "By what is Christian ethics to be distinguished from generally valid natural morality, if some theory of natural law becomes an authentic part and, to any degree, the primary foundation of Christian morality?"[10] This question is best answered by a counter-question: Why should we really want to distinguish Christian ethics from generally valid natural morality? I see nothing threatening in the possibility that the foundations of Christian morality may be the same as the foundations of the moralities associated with other faiths or with nonreligious beliefs. On the contrary, the more common ground Christians can find between their own ethical tradition and what Ramsey calls "generally valid natural morality," the better pleased they ought to be. For this means that there are a great many people who do not profess themselves Christians but who are nevertheless allied with Christians in their moral strivings and ideals. With them the Christian can cooperate with a good conscience—and not just as a tactical matter in some particular situation but because at bottom they share the same moral convictions.

Although Paul Lehmann identifies the end of the Christian with a true or mature humanity, he too attacks the notion of natural law and criticizes the idea of a philosophical ethic.[11] However, he does not enter into details of his objections to natural law, promising to do this in a future book. For the present, therefore, it is impossible to engage in a discussion with him on this matter.

A further objection made to the doctrine of natural law is that it does not take sin with sufficient seriousness. It assumes an innate tendency toward the good, failing to recognize the fallen condition of our human nature. I certainly have no wish to deny the fact of sin, and the question will be fully discussed later.[12] But I do not think of sin as having utterly destroyed the *imago Dei* or as having totally extinguished the drive toward authentic humanity. There is in man original righteousness as well as original sin, a tendency to fulfillment which is often impaired but never quite abolished; for if it were, the very consciousness of sin would be impossible.

Thus, although the idea of natural law is an unpopular one among many writers on Christian ethics today, their objections do not seem to be persuasive. Natural law, in some form, offers good hope of establishing a bridge between Christian ethics and general ethics. Indeed, I shall go further and claim that natural law is foundational to morality. It is the inner drive toward authentic personhood and is presupposed in all particular ethical traditions, including the Christian one.

What is natural law? The expression is ambiguous, and

misleading in many ways. Nowadays it might suggest to many people the uniformities of natural phenomena, though in this sense it is more customary to talk about "laws of nature." It is very important to make plain that natural law, as an ethical concept, is quite distinct from any scientific law of nature. It is true that some moral philosophers, especially those belonging to evolutionary and naturalistic schools of thought, try to derive moral laws from biological laws. It has sometimes been argued that in the course of evolution cooperation has proved more successful than competition, and it is inferred that one should therefore be altruistic.[13] But this rests on a confusion between the idea of law as uniformity and law as a norm of conduct which can be accepted and obeyed by a responsible agent. To put the matter in another way, the confusion is between what *is* the case and what *ought to be* the case. One cannot proceed from statements of fact to value judgments, unless indeed one has already smuggled a value-judgment into the alleged statement of fact, as when one says that cooperation is "more successful" than competition. Theodosius Dobzhansky seems to be correct in saying that what can be established biologically is not the content of an ethic but simply "the capacity to ethicize."[14]

We must therefore turn away from biological conceptions of natural law to the strictly ethical sense of the expression. The expression "natural law" refers to a norm of responsible conduct, and suggests a kind of fundamental guideline or criterion that comes before all rules or particular formulations of law. It will be useful to pass in review some of the classic historical statements concerning this idea.

Like natural theology, natural law has its roots in the Greek rather than in the Hebrew contribution to Christian and Western reflection. Perhaps the first trace of the doctrine is to be found in a somewhat obscure saying of Anaximander in which he talks of things "paying the penalty" and "making atonement to each other" for their injustice. Commenting on this saying, Werner Jaeger remarks: "Here is no sober rehearsal of the regular sequence of cause and effect in the outer world, but a world-norm that demands complete allegiance, for it is nothing less than divine justice itself."[15] Incidentally, this comment further clarifies the distinction between "law of nature" in the scientific sense and "natural law" in the ethical sense.

Another early Greek philosopher, Heraclitus, was much more explicit on the subject of a natural law. He tells us that "all human laws are nourished by the one divine law; for this holds sway as far as it will, and suffices for all and prevails in everything." Jaeger's comments[16] are again very illuminating. He points out that Heraclitus seems to have been the first to introduce explicitly the notion of law into philosophical discourse, and, in doing so, he identified "the one divine law" with the *logos,* the primordial word or reason in accordance with which everything occurs. "This theological aspect," claims Jaeger, "makes very clear how profoundly the law of Heraclitus differs from what we mean when we speak of a 'law of nature.' A 'law of nature' is merely a general descriptive formula for referring to some specific complex of observed facts, while Heraclitus' divine law is something genuinely normative. It is the highest norm of the cosmic process, and the thing which gives that process its significance and worth." Jaeger has some further interesting remarks on the reciprocal kind of interpretation done by the Greeks, who used social and human models such as law (*nomos*) to elucidate the cosmos and then in turn sought to throw light on social structures from the order of the cosmos. Such interpretation is not, of course, "merely circular," but can provide some useful reciprocal illumination.

Moving on to Aristotle, we read: "Law is either special [*idios*] or general [*koinos*]. By 'special law' I mean that written law which regulates the life of a particular community; by 'general law,' all those unwritten principles which are supposed to be acknowledged everywhere."[17]

Some of Cicero's remarks on natural law are worth quoting. He provides a more detailed statement than does Aristotle, and especially interesting from our point of view is his theological interpretation of natural law, viewed within the context of Stoic philosophy. He writes: "There is indeed a true law, right reason, agreeing with nature, diffused among all men, unchanging, everlasting. . . . It is not allowed to alter this law or to derogate from it, nor can it be repealed. We cannot be released from this law, either by the magistrate or the people, nor is any person required to explain or interpret it. Nor is it one law at Rome and another at Athens, one law today and another hereafter; but the same law, everlasting and unchangeable, will bind all nations at all times; and there will be one common lord and ruler of all men, even God, the framer and proposer of this law."[18]

According to St. Thomas Aquinas, "Among all others, the rational creature is subject to divine providence in a more excellent way, in so far as it itself partakes of a share of providence, by being provident both for itself and others. Therefore it has a share of the eternal reason, whereby it has a natural inclination to its proper act and end; and this participation of the eternal law in the rational creature is called the 'natural law.' "[19]

One last quotation comes from Richard Hooker, in the Anglican tradition. "The general and perpetual voice of men is as the sentence of God himself. For that which all men have at all times learned, Nature herself must needs have taught; and God being the author of Nature, her voice is but his instrument. By her from him we receive whatsoever in such sort we learn. Infinite duties there are, the goodness of which is by this rule sufficiently manifested, although we had no other warrant besides to approve them. The apostle

St. Paul, having speech concerning the heathen, saith of them, 'They are a law unto themselves.' His meaning is, that by the force of the light of reason, wherewith God illumineth everyone which cometh into the world, men being enabled to know truth from falsehood, and good from evil, do thereby learn in many things what the will of God is; which will, himself not revealing by any extraordinary means unto them, but they by natural discourse attaining the knowledge thereof, seem the makers of these laws which indeed are his, and they but only the finders of them out."[20]

A great many ideas are to be found in the passages quoted. The natural law is said to be unwritten; it is not invented by men but discovered by them; it is a kind of tendency rather than a code; it has a constancy or even an immutability. I certainly have no intention of attempting the defense of all the ideas contained in these quotations, even if they could be harmonized among themselves. But I do believe that something can and must be recovered from this pervasive notion of a natural law, and that it can be very relevant to some of our current problems. In the rest of the chapter, therefore, we shall try to see what is possible by way of reinterpretation and reconstruction.

The discussion will fall into two main parts. In the first, we shall consider the theological or ontological foundations of natural law and endeavor to interpret these in such a way that this law can indeed be seen as a common ground for the different ethical traditions. This discussion will inevitably raise in a provisional way the question of the relation between faith and morals, though the fuller examination of this will be deferred to later chapters. In the second part of the discussion, we shall consider what can be done toward reinterpreting natural law so that it takes account of the change and development which, as we have seen, are characteristic not only of man's images of himself but of his very nature and of the world around him.

1. It is acknowledged as a matter of fact that during most of the course of human history, religion and morals have been closely associated with each other. It is true that there have sometimes been religions with inhuman elements, practicing cruel and degrading rites. It is true also that there have been and are many highly moral persons who have disclaimed any religious convictions. Yet, on the whole, we are bound to say that the bond between religion and morals has been a close one.

How are we to understand this connection? Is it an intrinsic one, or is it merely an external and almost accidental one? Was it, for instance, appropriate that in the earlier stages of human development morals should be protected and inculcated by religion, but that as man becomes increasingly adult, morals should be detached from any connection with religion? This would parallel in the ethical field what has been true in many other fields of human activity, in which arts and sciences that were once pursued under the aegis of religion have become secularized and now flourish in complete autonomy.

Some of the traditional ways of explaining the bond between morality and religion were so inadequate and even repellent that, rather than stay with them, one would prefer to see morality break free from its religious associations. I refer especially to the view that religion provides the sanctions for morality and so the motivation for moral conduct, with its promise of reward for those who do good and its threat of punishment for evildoers. Such beliefs were widespread in ancient societies and persisted right down to the philosophers of recent centuries. John Locke could write: "The view of heaven and hell will cast a slight upon the short pleasures and pains of this present state, and give attractions and encouragements to virtue, which reason and interest, and the care of ourselves, cannot but allow and prefer. Upon this foundation, and upon this only, morality stands firm and may defy all competition."[21] Few people today believe in heaven and hell in the traditional sense, but they seem to be neither more nor less moral as a result. Even if there was the need for such a doctrine to buttress morality in earlier times, it would seem to have no place in the sophisticated societies of today. But more than this, I think we would say nowadays that to appeal to religion on the ground that it provides the sanctions for morality is to degrade both religion and morals. Religion is reduced to becoming a mere incentive to the moral life, while it is also suggested that men will not be moral apart from a system of ultimate rewards and punishments—surely a very cynical idea.

I believe that there is a connection between religion and morality, and that this connection is intrinsic and important. However, we must look for a way of interpreting it which will not do violence to the integrity of either religion or morality and that will not impugn the undoubtable achievements of secular morality. It can never be a question of subordinating religion to morality, or the other way around; nor can there be any question of claiming that morality is dependent on religious faith, in view of the plain fact that many nonreligious people are highly moral. Let me suggest, however, that natural law provides the link.

Though a religious faith is not to be identified with a metaphysic, it nevertheless always involves its adherents in some vision of the whole, in some fundamental convictions about "the way things are." Natural law too claims to be founded in "the way things are," in ultimate structures that are explicitly contrasted with the human conventions that find expression in our ordinary rules and customs. But natural law need not be given a theological or religious interpretation, and the conception of natural law is by no means incompatible with secular morality, and is indeed implied in some forms of it. Natural law is an ontological ground, common to the various forms of morality, receiving in some of them a religious interpretation, in others a secular. I would say that natural law (or something like it) is implicit wherever an unconditioned moral obligation is recognized. Perhaps this is implicit even in Camus, for in an absurd world it is apparently not absurd to be moral and to pursue the fulfillment of humanity.

That most people do seem to believe in something like natural law may be seen from a simple consideration. There is no human law, not even that promulgated by the highest authority, about which someone may not complain that it is unjust. There seems to be found among most people the conviction that there is a criterion, beyond the rules and conventions of human societies, by which these may be judged.

Every social group or association has some rules. These will normally be founded on the convenience of the members. If someone finds these rules unfair, and is unable to persuade the group to change them, he may have recourse to some superior set of laws to which the group itself is subject. There is always, so to speak, a higher court of appeal, a hierarchy of justice. There may be appeals through a whole series of courts, but even when the highest court of appeal has pronounced its judgment, it still makes sense for someone to say that its ruling was unjust. It is hard to see how this could be the case if justice has a purely empirical origin, explicable in terms of sociology, psychology, biology, and similar sciences.

Some jurists have held that the state is the ultimate source of law, so that what it decrees is *ipso facto* just and right— a theory, incidentally, which is no more arbitrary than the belief that what God decrees is therefore right. Such a positive theory of law, which was grounded in the state, was held in recent times by Nazi jurists in Germany. The state (or nation) was, for the Nazi, absolute. But most people would hold that there is an even more ultimate standard than the state, and that the state's laws and decrees can be unjust. According to Vernon J. Bourke, West Germany, Italy, and Japan are countries which have made considerable use of the natural law concept in reconstructing their legal and political institutions in the years following World War II.[22] It is surely significant that the three countries named were precisely lands that had for a time totalitarian rule. The concept of natural law is, among other things, a safeguard against the usurpation by the state of unlimited power.

Sophocles provided a dramatic account of the conflict between the laws of the state and the demands of "natural" justice:

CREON: Now, tell me thou—not in many words, but briefly— knewest thou that an edict had forbidden this?
ANTIGONE: I knew it. Could I help it? It was public.
CREON: And thou didst indeed dare to transgress that law?
ANTIGONE: Yes, for it was not Zeus that had published me that edict; not such are the laws set among men by the Justice who dwells with the gods. Nor deemed I that thy decrees were of such force, that a mortal could override the unwritten and unfailing statutes of heaven. For their life is not of today or yesterday, but from all time, and no man knows when they were first put forth.[23]

This scene from Greek tragedy antedates by some five hundred years a scene in the New Testament in which it is reported: "Then Peter and the other apostles answered and said: 'We must obey God rather than men.' "[24]

Of course, both of these excerpts, like the one quoted from Cicero earlier, are explicitly theological in what they say about the "higher law," and we should clearly understand that a doctrine of natural law does not necessarily commit one to a theistic belief. Governments which allow conscientious objection to military service only on *religious* grounds are acting unjustly. Indeed, one might even argue that to explain natural law or fundamental morality in terms of a divine Lawgiver is the most primitive and mythological way of expressing the idea. In the Old Testament, Moses receives the Decalogue, the basic laws of human conduct, at the hands of Yahweh. Likewise Hammurabi is depicted in Babylonian art as receiving the law from the god Marduk. In more recent times the natural law has sometimes been understood as the "will of God." But in such cases, God has been conceived on the deistic model, as an absolute monarch in the heavens. The natural law is not the "will of God," if this is understood to mean that God's arbitrary decree determines right and wrong. Men have sometimes complained that God has been unjust to them. Their complaints may have been unfounded, but it is interesting that such complaints can even be made, for it indicates that those who make them do not identify justice simply with what God wills. Justice is such an ultimate notion that it cannot depend even on the will of God. This does not mean that it is more ultimate than God, but rather that it is not external or subsequent to God, for it belongs to his very being or nature.

The point has been put so clearly by E. L. Mascall that I can do no better than quote some sentences from him: "To the Scotists, who taught that the formal constituent of God was infinity and that will was essentially superior to intellect, it was natural to say that the moral law rested simply on the arbitrary decree of God and that actions are good because God has commanded them; to the Thomists, on the other hand, it was *being* that was fundamental, with the necessary corollary that the moral law is neither an antecedent prescription to which God is bound by some external necessity to conform, nor a set of precepts promulgated by him in an entirely arbitrary and capricious manner, but something inherently rooted in the nature of man as reflecting in himself, in however limited and finite a mode, the character of the sovereign Good from whom his being is derived. The moral law is thus in its essence neither antecedent nor consequent to God; it is simply the expression of his own self-consistency. To say, therefore, that God is bound by it is merely to say, from one particular angle, that God is God."[25]

In any case, it would be hard to imagine a more abused phrase than "the will of God." People have committed all kinds of wickedness and folly in the belief that they were carrying out the will of God. In milder but no less objectionable ways, they still pressure other people into adopting their policies by representing their own idiosyncrasies as God's will which it would be wrong to disobey—a favorite tactic in ecclesiastical debates. How right Ian Henderson was when he wrote: "To enthrone the will of God in ecclesiastical party politics is to drive out love. For the point in calling your party policy the will of God is just that it enables you to give hell to the man who opposes it. For does that not make him the enemy of God? And what a wonderful opportunity to enable you, Christian that you are, to give vent to all the lovelessness in your nature."[26] Can we be surprised if many decent secular people are suspicious of any attempt to relate morality to any transcendent reality?

Yet we have seen that most people do indeed appeal to a "natural justice" beyond any human court of appeal. The Christian theologian will no doubt seek to link this notion eventually to his concept of God, but he will do so in more sophisticated ways than by the traditional appeal to the will of God. But it is possible to hold a natural law doctrine without giving it a theological formulation, though hardly without some ontological or metaphysical formulation. For the Stoics, the natural law was understood in somewhat pantheistic terms, as the demand of the *logos* dwelling both in man and in the cosmos. Likewise, in Eastern religions, the Hindu *dharma* and the Chinese *tao* are immanent and impersonal principles, not the decrees of a transcendent deity. In modern Western philosophy, one would be more likely to found natural law on a Kantian or neo-Kantian basis of an objectively valid rational order, which grounds moral values just as it does logical values. In each case, the foundations are taken to have an ultimacy and objectivity about them. They are not just "human convention," explicable psychologically, sociologically, and anthropologically. These sciences do explain the actual empirical forms in which morality appears, but not the ultimate demand of morality. Not even the state and not human society as a whole (if this expression refers to anything) can serve as the foundation of morality, but a transhuman order so that, as Hooker expressed it, man is not so much the maker of laws as their discoverer.[27]

Though the acknowledgment of a natural law that judges every human law does not, as we have readily agreed, imply a definitely theistic understanding of the world, nevertheless it points to an ontological interpretation of morality which has at least some kinship with the religious interpretation. For, in both cases, it is supposed that moral values do belong to the very nature of things, so to speak, and are not just superimposed on an amoral reality by the human mind. But surely to recognize that morality has this ontological foundation is already to perceive it in a new depth. Without such a depth, it is hard to see how there could ever be an unconditioned obligation to which one simply could not say no without abandoning one's authentic personhood. There could be only relative obligations, imposed by the conventions of a particular society. Conversely, as has been pointed out by Fritz Buri, where there is no ontological or religious grounding of morality, there is also no sin and "one can speak only of relative but not of unconditioned evil."[28] The Nazi regime, when man (or superman) decided moral values, should remain as a terrible warning against that complete slide into relativism and subjectivism in which morality has been entirely cut adrift from an ontological basis. The notion of human responsibility and answerability, when explored in its many dimensions, implies an order which man does not create but which rather lays a demand on him.

Although therefore one must nowadays abandon such oversimplified and frequently misleading notions as that the moral law is the will of God or that religion provides sanctions for strengthening the moral law, this does not lead to abandoning all belief in an intrinsic connection between morals and religion; and one can, moreover, see a parallel to such a religious morality in a secular morality which acknowledges a natural law. In both cases, if morality is founded in "the way things are," as natural law doctrine has maintained and as religious faith has maintained, then the moral demand has about it an ultimate character that can hardly fail to let it be experienced with an enhanced seriousness.[29]

2. In the second part of our discussion, we have to take up the question of how far the traditional idea of natural law can be adapted to the thinking of an age whose concepts are dynamic rather than static. So far we have talked of "unconditioned demand" and have sought a stable foundation for morality that could safeguard us from the vagaries of a thoroughgoing relativism. But it is equally important, in the light of our earlier discussions about man, to try to reinterpret the idea of natural law in a way that allows for flexibility and growth, so that it really does protect and foster the fulfillment of human possibilities. Are we perhaps asking the impossible? Demanding elements of both constancy and stability, while also wanting to acknowledge the pervasiveness of change and to set everything in motion? Or is there a way of embracing both sides?

First of all, I think we should be clear about what we are looking for. We are not looking for some extended system of rules. Just as the substance of faith can never be adequately or precisely formulated in dogmatic propositions, and just as all such propositions have time-conditioned elements that need to be expressed in new and different ways in new historical situations, so the content of the moral life is never exhaustively or adequately formulated in rules and precepts.

The fact that natural law cannot be precisely formulated is already implied in some of the classic definitions and descriptions quoted above. The natural law is "unwritten" (Aristotle). In fact, the very term "law" is misleading, if it is taken to mean some kind of code. The natural law is not another code or system of laws in addition to all the actual systems, but is simply our rather inaccurate way of referring to those most general moral principles against which particular rules or codes have to be measured. It is well known that St. Thomas formulated the first precept of the natural law in extremely general terms: "Good is to be done and promoted, and evil is to be avoided."[30] At first sight, one might be tempted to ask whether this statement says anything or is just a tautology, in the sense that it simply repeats what is already contained in the notions of "good" and "evil." I think, however, we shall find there is more to it than this.

It is assumed that one can go on to elaborate other precepts of the natural law, though these would be of a general kind. Perhaps we could reckon among them the very broad prohibitions which, as we have seen,[31] Bishop Robinson accepts as possessing something approaching universal validity. But the really important point in Robinson's statement has to do not with the actual prohibitions which he lists but with the fact that the prohibited activities are all, as he says, "fundamentally destructive of human relationships."

The Decalogue, setting forth the basic demands of the moral life, might be taken as a kind of transcript of the fundamental precepts of natural law, even though the

Decalogue itself is supposed to have been "revealed." But simple and basic though the Ten Commandments are, one finds even in them relative and time-conditioned elements. What, for instance, is one to say about the command concerning Sabbath observance?[32] Even with so basic a statement of the fundamental moral laws, there can be disputes as to what really belongs to natural law and what to the historical circumstances under which the statement was formulated. This reinforces our point that the natural law cannot be formulated, and that it is not so much itself a "law" as rather a touchstone for determining the justice or morality of actual laws and rules.

We may consider a more recent example. Sir David Ross lists some half-dozen *prima facie* duties, as he calls them: duties of fidelity (such as promise-keeping and truth-telling), duties of reparation, duties of gratitude, duties of justice, duties of beneficence, duties of self-improvement, and, negatively, the duty of not injuring others. These duties are called *prima facie* to allow for the situational element in morality. In an actual situation, there may be more than one claim on me, and then one has to take precedence over the other. But it is assumed that everyone is aware of the *prima facie* claims and that they are distinct from my fallible personal opinions about more peripheral ethical questions. "The main moral convictions of the plain man," writes Ross, "seem to me to be, not opinions which it is for philosophy to prove or disprove, but knowledge from the start."[33] I am inclined to agree with Ross that there is this kind of fundamental moral knowledge, given with human existence itself. Although he does not use the expression "natural law," I would think it quite appropriate. Furthermore, I would doubt whether the natural law could be particularized much beyond the half-dozen or so general duties which Ross details. And even these are *prima facie* duties, which may be superseded in an actual situation.

We have dwelt at some length on the difficulty of formulating the natural law with any precision and have seen that time-conditioned elements enter into such formulations as there are, and situational elements into its actual application. To this extent, we have already come into conflict with some of the classic descriptions of natural law, especially in their use of such words as "everlasting" and "unchangeable." But we are only at the beginning of our criticism. The notions of change and development have to be taken much more seriously than just allowing that there are changes and development in formulation. The notion of the unchangeableness of natural law was rooted in the idea of an unchanging nature, both in man and in the cosmos.

But if we acknowledge—as we already have done—that man's nature is open, and that he is always going beyond or transcending any given state of himself; and if we acknowledge further that this open nature of man is set in the midst of a cosmos which is likewise on the move and is characterized by an evolving rather than a static order; then we must say that the natural law itself, not just its formulations, is on the move and cannot have the immutability once ascribed to it. But what has perhaps more than anything else discredited the natural law concept is the tacit assumption that there was a kind of original human nature to which everything subsequent is an accretion. This is the confusion of what is natural with what is primitive. One has only to ask the question, "Is it natural to wear clothes?" to see the absurdity of trying to think of man's nature in terms of a primitive given. It is certainly futile to try to erect rules or maintain prohibitions on the basis of a "nature" that has long since been transcended. Man's very nature is to exist, that is to say, to go out of himself, and in the course of this he learns to take over from crude nature and to do in a human (and humane) way what was once accomplished by blind natural forces (both in man and outside of him) working in a rough and ready manner. An obvious example is population control, which need no longer be left to the hazards and diseases of nature without or to the tribal warfares prompted by the aggression of nature within. We have got beyond that kind of nature, and as I claimed in our discussion of man, the pill and the condom are now part of his nature.

But in admitting this, have we not cut away any ground for the other side of our argument concerning natural law? How can natural law provide a kind of criterion for evaluating particular laws? If this natural law is itself variable, can there be any reliable criterion at all? Or is everything reduced to relativism, subjectivism, and pragmatism?

I think we do still have a criterion, but its constancy is not that of a law but of a direction. So again we have to say that the word "law" is not entirely appropriate to describe the kind of thing traditionally meant by "natural law." What is meant is rather a constant tendency, an inbuilt directedness. To think of nature in dynamic terms is not to abandon all structure and reduce everything to flux. Although we talk much nowadays about change—and some people even talk about the "celebration of change"—it need hardly be said that change can be for the worse as well as for the better. The only kind of change we might want to celebrate would be change for the better. Teilhard de Chardin uses the expression "genesis" as a more precise way of saying what is meant. "In Teilhard's mind," writes Christopher Mooney. "we are not simply face to face with 'change' in the world but with 'genesis,' which is something quite different. . . . The word applies to any form of production involving successive stages oriented toward some goal."[34]

The movement that is envisaged, whether we are thinking of human nature or of cosmic nature, is a movement with direction, an ordered movement. But the movement in the cosmos is very different from the movement in man. The first kind of movement is unconscious evolution; the second has become a conscious moral striving. This corresponds to the difference between "laws of nature" and "natural law" in an ethical sense.[35] We should be quite clear that what we are talking about has nothing to do with the doctrine of an automatic progress of the human race, or with any complacent optimism. As soon as the transition is made from natural evolution to man's responsible self-development, the movement becomes subject to the risks of moral choice and to the actual reversals of sin. It is not like the unfolding of an oak from an acorn. This is something that happens, but in the case of man's development, it is a question about what *ought* to happen. At least in general terms, we know where we *ought* to be going, and we experience guilt when we go in some other direction. We know where we ought to be going because to exist as a human being is to exist with a self-understanding. This is an understanding both of who we are and of who we might become. It involves an image which summons us. To employ theological language for a moment, we might speak of the *imago Dei* both as fundamental endowment and as ultimate goal. Natural law is, as it were, the pointer within us that orients us to the goal of human existence. Actual rules, laws, and prohibitions are judged by this "unwritten law" in accordance with whether they promote or impede the movement toward fuller existence. Natural law changes, in the sense that the precepts we may derive from it change as human nature itself changes, and also in the sense that man's self-understanding changes as he sharpens his image of mature manhood. But through the changes there remains the constancy of direction.

This dynamic understanding of natural law is already implicit in St. Thomas' talk about the rational creature's having "a natural inclination to its proper act and end," while his awareness of the difference between a merely natural development in the world and man's conscious self-development is shown by his acute observation about the difference between a general providence in the world and the creature which has become itself provident.[36]

The directedness of moral striving has a constancy which prevents any lapse into sheer relativism. Even the relativisms of actual historical moral codes have often been exaggerated. Patrick Nowell-Smith claims that the more we study moral codes, the more we find that they do not differ in major principles.[37] All have the same direction, as it were. They aim at the development of a fuller, richer, more personal manhood, and to this extent they are in accord with and give expression to the natural law.

The Christian, we have seen, defines mature manhood in terms of Jesus Christ, and especially his self-giving love. But Christ himself is no static figure, nor are Christians called to imitate him as a static model. Christ is an eschatological figure, always before us; and the doctrine of his coming again "with glory" implies that there are dimensions of christhood not manifest in the historical Jesus and not yet fully grasped by the disciples. Thus discipleship does not restrict human development to some fixed pattern, but summons into freedoms, the full depth of which is unknown, except that they will always be consonant with self-giving love.

But the "natural" understanding of morality leads to conclusions not far from those of the Christian. For if man's nature is to *exist*, then he exists most fully when he *goes out* of himself. Here we strike upon the paradox of the moral life, perceived in many traditions—that the man who would "save" his life, that is to say, preserve it as a static possession, actually loses it, whereas the man who is prepared to venture out beyond himself and even to empty himself attains the truest selfhood.[38]

The discussion of this chapter, focusing on the concept

of natural law, suggests that there is no conflict between the ideals of a Christian ethic and the moral ideals to be found in humanity at large. Rather, there is a fundamental similarity. Christianity does not establish a new or different morality, but it makes concrete, clarifies, and, above all, focuses on a particular person, Jesus Christ, the deepest moral convictions of men. Christ declared he was fulfilling the law. not abolishing it.[39] According to W. D. Davies, even the so-called "antitheses" in the Sermon on the Mount (those passages in which Christ explicitly contrasts his own moral teaching with that of the Mosaic law) do not annul the law but carry it to "its utmost meaning."[40] It is obvious that this view of the matter agrees very closely with the one expounded here. Christian moral teaching is an unfolding of the "natural" morality of all men.

What for want of a better name has usually been called "natural law" is still a very useful concept. We have seen that it provides a firm basis for moral cooperation and community between Christians and non-Christians. We have seen further that natural law, even if it is not explicitly interpreted in theistic terms, nevertheless allows us to see moral obligation in a new depth, as ontologically founded. It safeguards against moral subjectivism and encourages moral seriousness by locating the demand of moral obligation in the very way things are.

5 Conscience, Sin, and Grace

From the consideration of law, we turn to examine the phenomenon of conscience. Its discussion will lead us further into the problem of the relation of morals and religious faith, and, in particular, it will raise the question of whether such traditional theological ideas as those of sin and grace still have relevance for the understanding of ethics, or whether, as some secular moralists maintain, such ideas can be only confusing.

As it is usually understood, conscience is a kind of built-in ✓ monitor of moral action, an interiorized law, as it were. But just as we have found it necessary to distinguish between actual codes of law and a "natural law" which underlies them, so it is possible to distinguish several levels of conscience. At its most concrete, conscience wrestles with some particular occasion of choice and decides on the right course of action in that situation. We can also think of conscience in a broader way as a more generalized knowledge of right and wrong, of good and bad. Moral theologians have sometimes used the expression "synderesis," or "synteresis," for this knowledge of general moral principles, but while it has been useful to distinguish it from the concrete exercise of conscience, there seems to be little point in retaining such an archaic and uncertain term, and it should probably be dropped from use. There is, I believe, still another level of conscience. It can be understood as a special and very fundamental mode of self-awareness—the awareness of "how it is with oneself," if we may use the expression. It is with this third level of conscience that we shall be mainly concerned.

However, the three levels should not be too sharply marked off from each other, for there is obviously continuity among them. This means also that the scheme could be further complicated if we were to take note of intermediate levels among the three that have been mentioned; for instance, between the knowledge of general moral principles and concrete conscientious deliberation over a particular question, there will be the intermediate knowledge of a particular code or set of rules. In this, the general principles are not only broken up into more specific prescriptions but are colored and interpreted by social and historical conditions.

St. Paul acknowledged a basic universal knowledge of moral principles when he wrote: "When Gentiles who have not the law do by nature what the law requires, they are a law to themselves, even though they do not have the law. They show that what the law requires is written on their hearts, while their conscience also bears witness and their conflicting thoughts accuse or perhaps excuse them."[1] Paul seems to be arguing here that even when there is no knowledge of the actual formulations of the law of Moses, there is a knowledge of moral principles (a law "written on their hearts") which may well issue in the same kind of conduct as is required by the law of the Old Testament, supposedly a law revealed directly by God. When Paul speaks explicitly of conscience in the passage quoted, it seems to me that he is thinking not just of a knowledge of general moral principles but of that further level of conscience, that fundamental mode of self-awareness that belongs to man's existential constitution and that "bears witness" as to how it is with him. Conscience is more likely to "accuse" than to "excuse." Yet the fact that we can be accused from the depth of our own being points to the presence there of an image or self-understanding that is being violated by our actual condition and demands that another condition ought to be realized.

Although Paul no doubt believed that the actual detailed precepts of the Jewish law were divinely given, nowadays we would be more likely to think of this complicated system of laws and rules as very much historically and socially conditioned; and if we recognized any law as having a claim to be considered "divine," it would consist in the underlying general moral principles. On one of its levels, however, conscience is formed by actual codes that bear all the marks of a particular historical and social context. These codes, moreover, are taught by parents, teachers, clergy, and others, who stamp them with still further idiosyncrasies of emphasis and interpretation. The kind of conscience that is formed by the inculcation of some particular code would seem to be the phenomenon that Sigmund Freud had in mind when he described the superego: "The long period of childhood during which the growing human being lives in dependence on his parents leaves behind it a precipitate, which forms within his ego a special agency in which this parental influence is prolonged. It has received the name of 'superego.' . . . The parents' influence naturally includes not only the personalities of the parents themselves but also the racial, national and family traditions handed on through them, as well as the demands of the immediate social *milieu* which they represent."[2] Conscience, then, understood as the superego, reflects the standards of a particular society or even a segment of a society, and conformity to these standards is required if one is to be acceptable in that society. So conscience in this sense would seem to have a considerable admixture of more or less narrow social conventions along with its basic moral insights, and it is presumably these conventions that people have in view when they speak disparagingly of "bourgeois morality," "Victorian taboos," the "Protestant work ethic," and the like.

Of course, the superego is a real and important phenomenon. But it does not account for more than some aspects of the complex phenomenon of conscience, and certainly not for the more important aspects. Actually, more recent psychoanalytic theory has recognized the importance for conscience of the so-called "ego-ideal"—a positive image toward which man transcends himself, in the manner we have earlier described.

We must therefore try to understand better those deeper levels of conscience which will sometimes sit in judgment on the pronouncements of a person's own superego (that is to say, the standards of his own society or social group) and may decide that they are inadequate or regressive. He may experience a lot of pain and guilt feeling before he can break away from them, but the fact is that some people do break away. Their very consciences, shall we say, are accused by a deeper level of conscience.

We have already entertained the suggestion that conscience is most radically understood as a fundamental mode of self-awareness. The Latin *conscientia* and the Greek *syneidesis* both signified "consciousness" in a general sense before they came to indicate specifically the moral consciousness. The basic function of conscience is to disclose us to ourselves. Specifically, conscience discloses the gap between our actual selves and that image of ourselves that we already have in virtue of the "natural inclination" toward the fulfillment of man's end.

Thus, conscience is not merely a disclosure; it is also, as

Heidegger insists,[3] a call or summons. It is a call to that full humanity of which we already have some idea or image because of the very fact that we are human at all, and that our nature is to exist, to go out beyond where we are at any given moment. Although we commonly think of conscience as commanding us to *do* certain things, the fundamental command of conscience is to *be*. What we do in any particular situation depends on what we seek to be, and, to this extent, ethical questions are dependent on ontological questions.

It will sometimes be the case that the summons of the authentic conscience will conflict with the standards of the conventional conscience, that is to say, the superego of Freudian analysis. We may think of this conflict as standing in analogy to the way in which the natural law may clash with some particular code of law. But, especially when the clash takes place on the level of the individual conscience, there is always grave danger of self-deception and perversion of conscience. There is a tendency nowadays to speak always disparagingly of "conventional morality" and of the "overstrict superego." But one has to be careful to inquire whether the criticism or rejection of the conventional standards is really based on a clearer conscientious insight or whether it flows simply from individual preference or veiled self-interest.

While undoubtedly there are occasions when the individual must heed his own conscientious convictions, no individual is a superman (*Übermensch*) so that he may lightly overrule the commonly accepted moral standards of his society. We have again to remind ourselves that the Nazis did this, with disastrous results. Friedrich Nietzsche offered a number of reasons for setting aside conventional morality, but the said reasons are frighteningly inadequate. According to him, ordinary morality derives its power from three factors: "the instinct of the *herd*, opposed to the strong and the independent; the instinct of all *sufferers* and *abortions,* opposed to the happy and well-constituted; the instinct of the *mediocre,* opposed to the exceptions."[4] Nietzsche's criticisms of conventional morality may be correct, but they set aside compassion and open the door to the possibility of ruthless exploitation and inhumanity.

At this point we come up against a very serious difficulty. On the one hand, conflict between the existential conscience and the conventional conscience would seem to be inevitable in all who are not content to be mere conformists. Only because there are such conflicts can moral progress take place, and the accepted codes of morality become modified as some members of the society gain deeper insights and protest against the accepted standards. But how are they to guard against claiming as "deeper insights" what may in fact be only personal prejudices? No conscience is infallible, and perhaps in this area self-deception is harder to detect and overcome than anywhere else. No moral philosopher has shown more respect for conscience or assigned it a more important role than has Bishop Butler. Yet this same thinker, in his brilliant sermon "Upon the Character of Balaam,"[5] has also shown how subtly the conscience of a good man can be influenced and distorted by self-deception.

But the fact that conscience is fallible cannot be taken to mean that the commonly accepted moral standards must never be challenged. The difficulty is to be met by insisting again on the essential social dimension that enters into all human existence, so that the existent can be truly described as a being-with-others.[6] There can be no self-fulfillment for such an existent apart from the fulfillment of the community in which his existence is set. Thus, if his conscience ever leads him into conflict with the commonly accepted standards, he must first of all open his conscience to the judgment and counsel of his fellows. If he is a Christian, he will also open it to any teachings of the Bible and the church on the matter in question. Only when he has endeavored, to the utmost of his ability, to make allowance for his own tendencies toward distortion and egocentricity can a person justifiably set up his own conscience in opposition to the commonly accepted code. Even then, it is possible that he may be mistaken. But unless some individuals were prepared sometimes to take this risk, it is hard to see how any moral progress could take place.

But now we strike upon a new and greater difficulty. If we allow that conscience is a kind of interiorized law by which man is disclosed to himself and summoned to authentic selfhood, it does not follow that he will in fact obey the summons. It is hard to know whether anyone ever acts deliberately and directly against his conscience—he is much more likely to manipulate his conscience and to justify his action. This is to be expected, for if conscience directs us to authentic selfhood, then to go deliberately against it would seem to be equivalent to deciding to destroy oneself. But there are times when conscience has been clarified as far as possible and the direction which it indicates cannot be doubted or evaded, and yet it is not obeyed; for the agent may at such times experience a kind of moral impotence which prevents him from responding to conscience's demand. It is partly for this reason that conscience is more often experienced as "accusing" than as "excusing," to use St. Paul's terminology. It is Paul himself who furnishes a classic description of the situation that we have in mind: "I do not understand my own actions. For I do not do what I want, but I do the very thing I hate. . . . I can will what is right, but I cannot do it. For I do not do the good I want, but the evil I do not want is what I do."[7]

Paul's words are a useful reminder that the moral life is neither so simple nor so easy as it is sometimes represented to be. But, more than that, the description of his experience brings us to face a crucial paradox of the moral life—a paradox so sharp that unless we can offer some solution to it, it threatens to reduce morality to absurdity. For what is the point of all our talk about law and conscience if in fact men cannot follow them? If conscience directs someone to a particular course of action, and if this person assents to his conscience and desires to follow its bidding, but in fact he finds himself doing something else, how can we talk of moral action at all, or what sense does it make to recommend one course of action rather than another?

There is universal agreement among moral philosophers that a moral act, as distinct from a mere occurrence like the falling of a snowflake, is characterized by both freedom and knowledge on the part of the agent. The agent is free, in the sense that he is not completely determined to act in the way he does, either by external circumstances or by internal drives. He acts with knowledge, both moral knowledge of what is right and wrong, and factual knowledge of what he is doing and the circumstances under which he is doing it. But if one can say, "I do not understand my actions," or, "I meant to do one thing and found myself doing another," as we find Paul saying, then how can we talk of moral action? Yet Paul clearly supposes that his actions did have moral quality—they were his own actions and he apparently felt guilty about them.

There can be no doubt that he does describe a state of affairs by no means uncommon. Conscience summons with its ultimate demand, yet in the face of this demand there is an impotence to act, a kind of inertia or pull in another direction, stultifying the good intention. This frustrating possibility drives us to ask whether man's moral strivings and aspirations make sense or are finally absurd, as so many "useless passions," in Sartre's language. If morality is to be taken seriously, then, in Kantian terms, "ought implies can." It makes no sense to say people ought to act in a certain way if they cannot. Yet, often enough, it seems to be just the case that they cannot.

The problem of whether and how one can make sense of the moral life brings us once more to the border of theology and ethics. The paradox can be resolved only if it can be shown that the moral life has a more complex and dialectical structure than is often supposed. I am going to suggest that such a structure is brought into view by a consideration of the theological notions of sin and grace. Although these notions have frequently been criticized by secular moralists, I think they can be expounded in ways that are not inimical to the integrity of secular morals, and one can even show that what the theologian calls "sin" and "grace" have parallels in nonreligious experience.

However, it must frankly be admitted that sin and grace are religious or theological ideas, and that the suspicion of the secular moral philosopher about the introduction of such ideas into ethical discussion has some justification. Yet, although sin and grace have primarily a theological import, they can be interpreted in a broader fashion. In relation to the moral situation and its demand, "sin" may be understood as the *disabling* factor that sometimes prevents the appropriate response to the demand; while "grace" is the *enabling* factor that sometimes permits the response to take place. I shall try to show that when we allow for the complexities introduced by these ideas, we shall be able to make sense of those perplexing situations in which, as it seems, ought no longer implies can, and the whole moral enterprise is threatened with a breakdown into absurdity.

However, we must first of all pause to consider the objections which moral philosophers might make to bringing such theological ideas as sin and grace into a discussion about ethics. Both of these ideas seem, in some way, to imply that man is not completely the master of his actions and that his moral life is not fully autonomous. But how can there be moral action, properly so called, unless it is free? And how can it be free if man's capacity to act is either disabled, so that he cannot do the good, or else must be enabled, so that the act would then seem to be not really his own? The moral philosopher could argue that the notions of sin and grace are so far from making sense of the moral life that they finally destroy it. They seek to alleviate one contradiction by introducing an even more monstrous contradiction.

A powerful defense of the autonomy of ethics against theological encroachments has been made in recent years by W. G. Maclagan.[8] He points out that many theologians of our time (Barth, Brunner, and Niebuhr are mentioned in particular) have held that man is rendered incapable through sin of either right action or even right thinking; and that, conversely, they have argued that whatever morally good action a man does must be accounted a work of grace. Such views, Maclagan believes, are destructive of the very meaning of morality. "The heart of the theology to which I am objecting is, as I understand it, the doctrine of *sola gratia,* the doctrine that what may be called 'natural man,' man apart from the work of grace, lacks the capacity to live as he should."[9] Maclagan's point is that if we accept such views, then there is no responsible human action—and therefore no morality—at all. "It is surely the case that, unless an act of will is in a quite unqualified sense a man's own work, there is nothing that can be his work even in a qualified sense and in some degree."[10]

Maclagan's objections are undoubtedly valid against some extreme views that have been put forward by Christian theologians, especially those working in the traditions of St. Augustine and John Calvin. If anyone gives credence to doctrines of either "total depravity" or "irresistible grace," then he does appear to deny the possibility of free responsible action, and he takes away any grounds for making a moral judgment on human conduct. Indeed, more than this, he really denies that man's being is truly personal. A man whose actions are already determined for him through his total subjection to sin or through his total possession by grace is a puppet, and so not a moral agent, for a puppet's activities are neither right nor wrong.

Christians ought also to consider how offensive the statements of some theologians must be to honest secularists who are striving hard to achieve an authentic human community. Who is going to have the effrontery to say that all their efforts are rendered nugatory by sin and that they will get nowhere without the grace that comes with Christian faith? It must be added that there is no convincing empirical evidence that would support these Christian—or supposedly Christian—assertions.

But if we allow that Maclagan has a valid case, are we then to accept a Pelagian view of the matter and say that man is always free to make a choice between good and evil or, at least, a choice between better and worse? I do not think we can say this either, for in fact our freedom is usually limited, and sometimes is reduced almost to the vanishing point. Our own past actions and the habits we have built up, the pressures and prejudices of society, and a great many other factors combine to push us toward actions that we would not really choose to do. Sin may be reckoned among these factors, or it may be the inclusive name for all of them taken together. It is not absolutely determinative of our action, but it pushes us one way rather than another. Moral realism has to recognize that in spite of high moral aspirations and the determination to follow them, there may be impotence to carry out the policies that are inwardly approved. So we seem to be driven back from the untenable position in which sin and grace are so interpreted that man is reduced to a puppet to the equally untenable, because self-contradictory, position, noted earlier, in which the moral demand of the ought is experienced but the capacity to respond to it is lacking. We seem to be caught in a disjunction in which we are unable to affirm either side.

Clearly, we must seek a more dialectical approach, one that will do justice to the valid insights that belong to each side of the disjunction. In fact, we do find in the theological tradition further ideas that can be helpful in leading toward a more adequate dialectic.

Some Christian theologians (myself included) have held that any doctrine of original sin needs to be counterbalanced by a doctrine of original righteousness.[11] In the biblical stories of the creation and the fall, man was created good before he fell into evil. So long as he remains man, some trace of this goodness remains also, if only in the form of an image of who he ought to be—an image that we have already linked with the notion of an *imago Dei*.[12] As Paul Ricoeur has expressed it, "However radical evil may be, it cannot be as primordial as goodness."[13] Evil is essentially secondary and parasitic, and it is doubtful whether there could be a "total depravity." Something of an original righteousness remains, even if it is heavily impaired by sin.

To acknowledge the reality of an original righteousness that persists along with original sin and is even more fundamental is also to acknowledge that there is a kind of grace in creation itself. We may call it, if we wish to use an expression sometimes employed in the history of theology, a "common grace." To be sure, "grace" and "nature" are relative terms, and some people might argue that a common grace belonging to creation itself is simply nature. But the use of the word "grace" expresses the giftlike character of that original righteousness or desire for the good, which is never extinguished in man. Existence itself is a gift, for we did not make ourselves, and in this sense there is a grace of existence, a grace that is prior to particular experiences of grace within a community or a religious faith.

In its treatment of sin and grace, much of our traditional theology has been guilty of a twofold distortion: it has laid more stress on original sin than on common grace; and it has tended to regard both sin and grace in objectified, mythological ways—sin as a kind of taint or stain, and grace as a kind of mysterious essence that is "infused" into the human soul or that somehow takes possession of a person's will.

As against this distortion, we must advance a contrary twofold claim: that sin and grace are always present, and that they must be understood in nothing less than personal or existential terms. That is to say, while indeed they may support or deflect the agent, as the case may be, they do not infringe on his personal responsibility. In the theology of the Christian life, sin and grace constitute a dialectic within which responsible human action takes place. Something of this dialectic is expressed by St. Paul when he writes: "Work out your own salvation with fear and trembling, for it is God who works in you. . . ."[14] Yet, in talking of an original sin and of a common grace, I am also maintaining that the dialectic of sin and grace (even if it may not be called this) is not peculiar to the Christian life but characterizes all moral striving. Everywhere, enabling and disabling forces work upon the human will, though without destroying our ultimate personal responsibility. These enabling and disabling forces, wherever they are found, are akin to what the Christian calls "grace" and "sin." Since the Christian believes that grace is more primordial than sin, then, without denying or minimizing sin, he also maintains the essential hopefulness of the moral struggle. But of this we shall have more to say later.

Meantime, however, I may well be asked whether, in spite of all my protestations about not "annexing" the non-Christian, I am in fact infringing the integrity of his position by claiming that sin and grace are operative for him too. He would probably be ready enough to acknowledge a secular equivalent of sin, but is not grace too definitely a religious conception? In the lecture by Marxist philosopher Milan Mahovec quoted earlier,[15] he showed himself very ready to entertain notions of transcendence and mystery, excluded by classical Marxism but now being reconsidered in the dialogue with Christians. But he stated that the one Christian doctrine that he found impossible to accept was the doctrine of grace. One can understand the reason for this rejection if grace is understood—as in the *sola gratia* tradition—to mean that man's salvation is accomplished solely by God and that man is passive in the process; for such a doctrine would certainly give the Marxist good reason for supposing Christianity to be the "opium of the people." But I have explicitly rejected such an exaggerated account of grace. I would suggest to the secularist who is suspicious of the notion of grace that whenever he experiences thankfulness for the mystery of his existence, whenever an unexpected good supervenes in his experience, whenever he is "surprised by joy," to use C. S. Lewis' expression, he knows something analogous to what the Christian calls grace. One attributes this to God, the other does not, but for both it is indeed a mystery.

But let us undertake a closer analysis of sin and grace, and perhaps some further parallels between these theological ideas and secular experience will emerge. We consider sin first.

Sin has many faces and has been described in many ways —as taint, transgression, missing the mark, disobedience to law, imbalance, and so on. The many words and symbols that have been employed point to the diversity of ways in which the nature of sin has been understood.[16] I believe that what is possibly most basic to the notion of sin is the idea of separation or alienation. This sense of alienation can be experienced at various levels—alienation from oneself, alienation from one's fellows, alienation from society and its institutions, alienation from the whole "scheme of things" or from God. Conscience, as we have seen, discloses man as separated from his authentic self, and sin, as a religious conception, sees this separation as extending into the wider context in which the individual existent is placed, or even into that widest context in which society itself and human history are placed. Original sin is the disrupted context, already flawed and distorted, within which moral actions take place. Hell would be the final isolation and disintegration of the existent if the tendencies toward sin worked themselves out to their conclusion.

Incidentally, the Marxist would have much less trouble with the idea of sin than he has with that of grace. For one obvious difference between Marx and the nineteenth-century liberals was that, unlike the liberals, Marx believed in something like original sin (alienation) and therefore in the necessity of something like conversion (revolution).

We turn now to grace. If sin is expounded in terms of alienation and separation, then grace is to be understood as the overcoming of alienation and as the reconciling of what has been thrust apart. The very fact that sin can be experienced is itself an evidence of the priority of grace, for how could anyone be aware of being separated unless he already had the idea of a larger whole to which he rightly belongs? We may say that grace is at work wherever that which has become isolated and fragmented is incorporated into a larger whole, but incorporated in personal terms, rather than being merely absorbed or annexed into the whole. Grace, as thus conceived, is experienced in many ways: in the life of the individual, when isolated and conflicting impulses are integrated into a larger pattern, often without any conscious effort; again, when the individual existent finds his place in a community; finally, in the specifically religious sense, when human striving and effort cooperate with and are in turn strengthened by the larger strivings of history and of the whole creative process itself.

It is true that the notion of grace is an elusive one. It has been set forth in many ways in the history of Christian theology—and of other theologies besides, for it is not an exclusively Christian idea. Perhaps the many ideas of grace correspond to the many ideas of sin. I shall not attempt any correlation of particular ideas of grace with particular ideas of sin, but I shall briefly mention some of the principal ways in which Christians have thought of grace. There is *sacramental grace:* through the sacramental action, whether in baptism or in the eucharist, the individual is incorporated into the community and also into what is believed to be the transcendent source of the community's life. There is the *grace of forgiveness:* this understanding of grace is typical of the Protestant tradition, in which the preached word of reconciliation is aimed at freeing the hearer from the bonds of his past, and enables him to embark on a new life of obedience and cooperation. There is also the *grace of mystical union:* although this may be confined to exceptional individuals, it is not confined to the Christian tradition but is found in other religions and in some forms of philosophy, and those who know of themselves as participating in this kind of grace believe themselves to be joined directly to God, the world spirit, the cosmic *élan,* or however they may call it, so that they receive in their moral and spiritual strivings a dynamic from beyond themselves.

Whatever the theory of grace may be, the same broad kind of experience is indicated in each case. It is the experience of what we have called an "enabling" factor in the attainment of authentic life or, to put the matter in another way, of a supportive context within which the striving after the good takes place. Moreover, there is the conviction that grace overcomes the disruptive and disabling tendency of sin and is stronger than sin. We can agree with Joseph Fletcher when he describes the Christian ethic as a "eucharistic" ethic.[17] It is so in a double sense—it is an ethic of thanksgiving, and it is an ethic lived in the community of grace.

But I have made the claim that sin and grace, the disabling and enabling factors in the moral life, are known (though possibly by different names) in the moral life generally, as well as in Christian experience. Though sin and grace are primarily religious phenomena, something akin to them is widely diffused through human experience, and to recognize this is to form yet another bond between religion and morality, and between Christian and non-Christian ethics. I have already drawn attention to the connection between the Christian (or religious) idea of sin and the Marxist recognition of alienation; but the lostness and alienation that the religious man associates with sin has found very widespread expression in the twentieth century, especially in literature, in which man is often represented as having cut himself off not only from his own true being and community but somehow from the deeper roots of his life, from being itself, from the source of his existence, from "God," among those who use this language. On the other side, the support and enabling that come from friendship, love, the fact of belonging to a community—these are also widely known, and they form a counterpart to what the theologian calls "grace." But when we explore the depth and mystery of these interpersonal relations, do we not find ourselves compelled to say that mediated through them there is a "common grace" of existence that comes with the gift of existence itself? In holding that the "real world" is constituted for us chiefly by other persons, John Baillie has maintained that "if others are the real world, it is because they embody for me, in my encounter with them, something greater than themselves, an intrinsic right and a universal good."[18]

If then one is prepared to acknowledge that sin and grace are everywhere intertwined with the moral life, this life is seen to be much more complex in its structure than it appears when there is supposed to be simply a freedom of choice between good and evil or between better and worse. To recognize sin is to acknowledge the disabling factors that sometimes frustrate the most earnest moral striving. To recognize grace is to acknowledge what Matthew Arnold called "the power not ourselves making for righteousness." This is the power which proves stronger than the disruptive tendency and makes sense of moral endeavor. But this is also the power which Christians (and many others) have called "God."

It could be objected that in the preceding argument I have subsumed everyday experiences of alienation on the one hand and of moral strengthening on the other under the theological categories of sin and grace, whereas one could have proceeded in the opposite direction by subsuming supposedly religious experiences under everyday ones. Actually, I do not think I have so much tried to subsume the secular experiences under the religious ones as simply to set them alongside one another, to let them interpret each other, and to suggest that there is a deep-lying affinity between them. If, as a theologian, I have tended to make the theological categories primary, I have also acknowledged that these categories need a measure of demythologizing and that some of the traditional ways of understanding sin and grace are quite inadequate.

What I would certainly resist would be the attempt to account for all these matters in terms of a reductionist type of psychology. Let us acknowledge that an explanation in terms of a reductive naturalism is always possible. But I do not think that such an explanation does justice to the depth of human existence, of moral experience, and of inter-personal relations. Nor do I think that the reductionist approach does justice to contemporary secular accounts of man, for we have seen that these accounts are recognizing the elements of transcendence and mystery in man's being.[19]

Among the ways of talking about these matters, theology (or God-language) has its own difficulties, but it also has a long experience, a subtle vocabulary, and a rich symbolism. As Bishop Robinson has written, "It is a way of keeping guard over the irreducible, ineffable mystery at the heart of all experience."[20] We come especially close to this mystery in moral experience. To acknowledge the mystery of grace is to recognize both an ultimacy and a hopefulness in the moral life. One need not do this in specifically Christian terms, but wherever it is done, we seem to have something akin to a religious outlook on the world, at least an "open" humanism as distinct from a "closed" humanism. Bishop Robinson speaks of "the consciousness of being encountered, seized, held by a prevenient reality, undeniable in its objectivity, which seeks one out in grace and demand. . . . While the reality is immanent, in that it speaks to him from within his own deepest being, it is also transcendent, in that it is not his to command: it comes, as it were, from beyond him with an unconditional claim on his life. The fact that life is conceived as a relationship of openness, response, obedience to this overmastering reality, is what distinguishes the man who is constrained to use the word 'God' from the non-believing humanist."[21]

The support which religious faith and moral striving give to each other has been well expressed by H. J. Paton. He writes: "If a man believes that the supreme value in life, the one which claims priority above all others, is to do his duty; if he believes also that it is his supreme duty to live, so far as he may, as a free citizen of an ideal community, and

6   Hope and the Moral Dynamic

The essence of the Christian life has been traditionally described in terms of the so-called "theological" virtues, the triad of faith, hope, and love mentioned by St. Paul at the close of his great hymn on love.[1] Christian moral theologians set these three theological virtues alongside the four cardinal virtues of classical philosophy, wisdom, courage, temperance, and justice, and so produced a convenient total of seven. No doubt this was an artificial scheme, and yet it did seek to express some matters that are of concern to our own inquiry. In the first place, by using the term "virtues" for both groups, the qualities prized by the ancients and the qualities set forth as the crown of the Christian life, the moral theologians were acknowledging the continuity between the general moral striving of mankind and the specifically Christian moral aspirations. In the second place, in calling the cardinal virtues "natural" and the Christian virtues "theological," they were claiming that the moral life is strengthened and enriched by the addition of a religious or theological dimension.

It must be said, however, that the theological virtues are

badly named, just as we have seen that "natural law" too is an inadequate and misleading expression. It seems clear, for instance, that even if love could be regarded as a "virtue" of the same order as courage and wisdom, faith and hope seem to be qualities of a different kind. Faith and hope are not additional moral virtues, but rather attitudes that may accompany all the other moral virtues—attitudes which, I think it may be claimed, can strengthen these virtues and supply a moral dynamic. Of course, Paul seems to be saying that love or charity too can, and should, accompany all other virtues, but I would argue that love is of a very different nature from faith and hope, for the two latter virtues seem to imply beliefs of a kind which are either theological or, at least, on the way to becoming theological.

If the noun "virtue" is unsatisfactory when applied to the qualities named by Paul, the adjective "theological" is likewise misleading. Surely no one will claim that faith, hope, and love are found exclusively in the context of Christianity. They may indeed have a specifically Christian expression (and this may be what St. Thomas had in mind when he asserted that "these virtues are not made known to us save by divine revelation contained in Holy Scripture").[2] But faith, hope, and love are found also in other religions and in many forms of humanism. Love, in one form or another, is as universal as humanity itself. Faith and hope, I have said, seem to imply beliefs of a more or less theological kind, but perhaps I should broaden this statement and talk of beliefs of a more or less "ontological" kind, to allow for the real possibility of forms of faith and hope among persons who have no explicit theology. Their faith and hope may be based on beliefs about "the way things are," but these beliefs may not be Christian or even theistic in any conventional sense.

I have said that love, in one form or another, is a universal virtue among mankind. Some may reply that love, in the sense of *agape,* is a peculiarly Christian virtue. I would not wish to deny that the nuances of the Christian story may likewise produce nuances in the kind of love which it inspires, but I do not think that Christian belief produces a kind of love that is fundamentally different from the love that may be found among non-Christians. I have already indicated that it is obvious that love is not nearly as dependent on one's beliefs as faith and hope seem to be. Some theologians, of course, have tried to show that Christian love is of a quite unique kind, and in particular they have tried to differentiate the *agape* of the New Testament from the *eros* of classical philosophy.[3] But the distinction is by no means an absolute one, and we have already seen that an *agape* altogether separated from *eros* runs the risk of becoming a love without compassion.[4] I do not think it can be convincingly maintained that, as far as its basic characteristics are concerned, Christian love is of a unique kind having no parallels elsewhere.

The theological virtues then are not additional obligations or aspirations or excellences that belong exclusively to Christian morality, but, like sin and grace, they have their counterparts in all moral striving, even if it is in Christian theology that they have been specially brought into the focus of attention. Their function, as we shall see, is to promote attitudes that will affect our decision making and that will help to sustain the carrying out of moral policies. These attitudes bring a certain dynamic into the moral life, and they rest finally on theological (or ontological) insights. These may be more or less explicit, and they have to do with the wholeness and connectedness of the moral life within a wider context.

Our discussion will center mainly on hope. This takes up the theme on which we touched at the end of the last chapter, when H. J. Paton was quoted as pointing to the connection between a religious faith and the hopefulness that inspires moral striving. If anyone is going to embark with any enthusiasm on what Jürgen Moltmann calls a "transforming mission," then, according to Moltmann, he "requires in practice a certain *Weltanschauung*, a confidence in the world and a hope for the world."[5] The converse is stated by Pierre Teilhard de Chardin: "An animal may rush headlong down a blind alley or towards a precipice. Man will never take a step in a direction he knows to be blocked."[6] Hope that there is at least a chance of success seems to be indispensable to any human striving, but hope, in turn, rests on deep convictions about the universe in which human life is lived.

In centering the discussion on hope, I am not suggesting that hope can be separated from faith and love, and, indeed, the passages quoted point precisely to the relation of hope to faith. Feuerbach remarks: "Hope is only faith in relation to the future."[7] The "theology of hope" associated with Moltmann and others is almost a tautologous expression, for theology treats of God, and, in turn, the word "God," whatever else it means, points to an objective ground of hope in the way things are; it points to whatever it is that allows us to have "faith in Being."[8] This is the faith that there is some final worth and dignity in human existence, and that man's striving for a fuller existence is not doomed to frustration but is supported by the creative process itself.

Concerning the relation of hope to faith within the triad of theological virtues, Moltmann writes: "In the Christian life faith has the priority, but hope the primacy. Without faith's knowledge of Christ, hope becomes a utopia and remains hanging in the air. But without hope, faith falls to pieces, becomes a fainthearted and ultimately a dead faith. It is through faith that man finds the path of true life, but it is only hope that keeps him on that path."[9] But if, on the one side, faith establishes hope, then, on the other side, hope supports and nourishes love. As St. Paul says, "Love bears all things, believes all things, hopes all things, endures all things."[10]

I should explain more fully why the discussion of this chapter will be concentrated on the theme of hope, and how the relations of faith, hope, and love are to be understood. We are focusing attention on hope because hope seems to be a part of the relation between religion and morals that has not yet been considered in this book. It has to do with the question that came into view at the end of the preceding chapter, when it was claimed that moral striving needs a measure of hopefulness to supply it with dynamic. Of the other two theological virtues, faith is most closely connected with the themes treated in the chapter which dealt with natural law and the moral order, while love has to do primarily with the themes of grace and reconciliation, treated in the fifth chapter.

Emil Brunner somewhat oversimplifies the relations of faith, hope, and love when he relates them to the temporal dimensions of past, future, and present, respectively. He writes: "We live in the past by faith; we live in the future by hope; we live in the present by love."[11] In a very general way, and with many qualifications, it may be possible to make this statement. But past, present, and future are always together in personal existence, and the isolation of any one of them has bad consequences. For instance, a faith that relates only or even primarily to the past becomes a kind of traditionalism. Faith is also present attitude and commitment to the future. Nevertheless, faith does base itself on what is given, while hope, as "faith in relation to the future," moves into what is to come.

In saying that faith bases itself on what is given, I come back to the point that it is closely related to the themes treated in our discussion of natural law. Faith is acceptance of and commitment to Being or however we may name the ultimate reality that has brought forth human life. Faith

thus implies the conviction that there is a context of meaning and value prior to the meanings and values that we
create; and, for ethics, this implies that moral obligation is
rooted not merely in human convention but ontologically.
In terms of the Bible, these convictions of faith first find
expression in the doctrine of creation. Hence, especially in
the Lutheran tradition, the notion of natural law has been
closely associated with the order of creation. According to
Regin Prenter: "Creation and law belong together. In struggling against the powers of chaos, and in giving life to the
world, God sets up a law for all his creatures."[12] In the New
Testament the focus of faith shifts to Jesus Christ. He is
the initiator of the "new creation," the author of the "law
of Christ," the "measure of the stature" of mature manhood,
to use three appropriate expressions from the Pauline
epistles.[13] In each case, whether we are thinking of the
doctrine of creation or of the revelation in Jesus Christ, faith
has to do with something given, and implies that this provides a meaningful context for human life and for moral
striving now and in the future.

The theological virtue of love, on the other hand, is closely
connected with grace. In our discussion of sin and grace and
of the opposition between them, we saw that the work of
grace is to build up wholes out of fragments, to overcome
separations, to effect reconciliation. Grace was described as
the "enabling" factor in life, and we may say that the highest
form of love (the *agape* of the New Testament) is simply
enabling people to *be*. The assertion that "God is love"[14]
expresses the faith that the creative power of the universe
is also a reconciling power, seeking to bring all creatures
into ever fuller being. The command to love points man to
his obligation to take part in this creative and reconciling
work—a work which brings into being personality and community.

But how will this work end, and with what confidence

can we embark on it? It is here that the question of hope arises. The moral life builds on faith and love, but does it achieve? Do the strivings and sacrifices of men really make a difference in the world, or are they doomed to waste and frustration? The Christian virtue of hope is the confidence (if that is not too strong a word) that moral striving does attain. This virtue of hope is connected especially with the doctrine of eschatology, or the teaching concerning the last things. This teaching maintains that human history and likewise the whole cosmic process, of which our history is a small part, do have a goal and a directedness. They move, however painfully and—it would seem—uncertainly, toward a consummation, in which that striving after the good in which man engages and in which he may believe himself to be supported by the activity of God himself is increasingly brought to fruition. This consummation need not be considered final or static—it may well open the way to new consummations. But eschatological hope holds out the promise that what is now achieved only fitfully and ambiguously will eventually be manifested in its fullness. The hope is that the signs of the kingdom of God, the partial and fleeting realizations of the good that we see today, are not just sports or accidents in this world, but are indicators of its destiny. With this hope to encourage him, man, we may suppose, will be more eager and more persevering in his attempts to obey the command of love and build up the beloved community.

But may we really suppose so? Is hope truly a moral dynamic, or have allowed ourselves to become too sentimental in what we have been saying? Let me frankly acknowledge that the question is far from easy to answer.

Let us consider for a moment the extreme point of view found among those who believe that man has to create and pursue his own values in the midst of a cosmos that is alien to them, and that will probably in the end destroy them without trace. Some have gone even further, arguing that man's existential constitution is itself infected with absurdity, and the realization of his values would be as frustrating as satisfying. At one stage in his career Sartre could write that all human activities are "equivalent," and this was explained to mean that as far as their ontological status is concerned, they are all equally nugatory.[15] Admittedly, this is an extreme expression of nihilism. What would it do to the human will? Some people might grimly pursue the good even if convinced of the futility of their actions, but many others would fall into a moral paralysis, induced by a basic despair about the human condition. If man is inherently a contradiction and if his ideals are doomed to frustration, then why should anyone bother? Let us indeed make the best of a bad job and minimize the evils that afflict us, but let us also recognize that in the end it will not matter very much what one has done or failed to do.

Yet just at this point we come on the ambiguities of the situation. There are people who do not believe in any power making for righteousness in the world, who have no explicit hope that the world process is directed toward any meaningful end, who, to put it briefly, do not believe in God in any sense, and yet are not victims of the kind of moral paralysis which we have envisaged. Such persons are sometimes wholeheartedly devoted to moral and social ideals, and their ideals may be very close to those of the Christian religion. In particular, the writings of Albert Camus confront us with the phenomenon of the highest moral seriousness conjoined with the complete absence of eschatological hope.

Again, the Christian must be careful to resist the temptation to show that such persons are somehow crypto-believers. It is true that in some secular traditions there are quasi-theological elements which could be construed as affording a ground of hope. For instance, Marxism has its eschatology and, to this extent, is not correctly described as completely godless. But Camus is in a different category. Here we have the conscious rejection of hope, but likewise the rejection of resignation and indifference. Hope is replaced by rebellion; and "metaphysical rebellion is the movement by which man protests against his condition and against the whole of creation."[16]

We have already taken note that the "absurd hero" would be such an exceptional and paradoxical figure that he could hardly be significant for everyday ethical problems, and that it is hard to see why, if everything is absurd, one should take the morality of rebellion seriously.[17] Yet even if there is only a handful of such people, they present a serious challenge to all the underlying assumptions of a morality of hope. Are hope and faith merely devices for motivating ordinary people, while those with sufficient strength of character move beyond them? Is not the moral striving of a person devoid of ultimate hope to be judged as having more moral worth than the similar striving of a man who is encouraged by believing that he is helping to forward a process which is rooted in reality itself and is destined to come to fruition?

Such a judgment, incidentally, would have no relation to popular eschatology, with its expectation of rewards and punishments. It would hold even in the case of a Christian whose notion of "heaven" had been so purged of egocentric expectations that he could not be accused of doing the good for the sake of an extrinsic reward. An existentialist of the kind who would make the judgment we have in view would claim that the nihilist or the atheist, because he is pursuing the good in spite of his belief that what he accomplishes will turn out to be rather futile, is making a genuinely human and authentic choice; whereas the man who is motivated by the hope that morality belongs to the way things are and will really achieve is, in Sartre's phrase, in "bad faith," for he is allowing his action to be determined by extraneous circumstances. He is essentially a conformist, while the rebel, even if doomed to failure, is at least asserting himself.

Furthermore, if it is true that a nihilistic despair may, in many people, induce moral indifference, is it not equally true that an eschatological hope may do the same? According to Walter Rauschenbusch, the earliest Christians were not interested in social or political reforms because they believed that the world was speedily coming to an end and there was not much point in trying to improve it.[18] Even if nowadays eschatologically oriented theologies of hope have turned away from otherworldly apocalyptic, and understand the hope in more definitely historical and ethical terms, may not this very hope induce complacency, rather than serving as an incentive to action? If God is bringing his purposes to maturity, is it really important what we do, even if we acknowledge that "hominization" has brought man into the evolutionary process as an active responsible partner who can either hasten or obstruct the process? I sometimes hear such ways of talking among Christians, and whatever theological justification these ways of talking can claim, they can easily lead to a dulling of moral sensitivity and certainly to the elimination of any sense of urgency about our moral tasks today. I mean such talk as that the world is already redeemed, all men are already incorporated into Christ, and the like. Unless such talk is very carefully qualified, it can lead to a measure of moral complacency and even to a kind of smugness, and I have occasionally observed this.

Let us now briefly consider a concrete illustration which will serve to point up the ambiguities associated with the place of hope in the moral life. In one of his books John C. Bennett mentions that "Professor Morgenthau offers, as his ultimate rejection of nuclear war as a rationally chosen instrument of policy, his conclusion that such a war would destroy the meaning of life for the survivors who are secularists, who have no faith in God as transcending history."[19] This is an extremely interesting statement, and one could spend a long time discussing it. Presumably Morgenthau implies that Christians who survived would still have some hope and would still see meaning in life. But what does this say about the Christians? It might be taken to mean that the Christian survivors, still having hope, would set about the tasks of building anew with more moral energy than those for whom the meaning of life had been destroyed, as Morgenthau expresses it. This, in turn, might be taken as a confirmation of Moltmann's point, quoted above,[20] that the "transforming mission requires in practice a certain *Weltanschauung*." But one could read the situation in another way. The secularist might argue that the apparently invincible hope of the Christians and their retention of it after so great a disaster is the mark of moral insensitivity rather than of moral strength. The Christian, it might be said, still sees meaning in life when he really ought to be seeing its sheer horror and absurdity. Moreover, one can raise also at this point the question of falsifiability. What would need to happen to persuade the Christian that his hope was illusory? If nothing could destroy Christian hope, then one would have to ask whether there is sense any longer in a hope that seems to be compatible with any and every state of affairs.

To compound the ambiguity of this situation, it must be mentioned too that, in spite of Professor Morgenthau, some Christians do say that a nuclear war would destroy their belief in God and their eschatological hope. And some of them argue that after such a catastrophe only the secular humanist could still have a measure of hope, for he would not have become disillusioned about the nature of things, and he might well hope that man, with his astonishing resilience, could overcome this disaster as he has overcome so many in the past.

There are still other questions that can be asked about

hope—at any rate, of eschatological hope, the hope that history and indeed the whole cosmic process is headed for a meaningful goal. One may ask whether this vast hope is not simply a palliative for despair in the face of actual disappointments. Is eschatology an escape into dreams of the future, induced by unbearable present realities? It was precisely when the political fortunes of the Jewish people were at their lowest ebb that their apocalyptic expectations became most extravagant. Conversely, in the early Christian community, the once vivid eschatology faded into the background as the church established itself in the world.

I have somewhat labored the ambiguities of hope so that it will be plain to us, in this matter as in so many of the others we have considered, that oversimplified solutions will not suffice. Certainly, one cannot baldly assert that the Christian has hope and the atheist is in despair; and one cannot claim either that an eschatological hope is always a moral dynamic.

Yet, in spite of the ambiguities and possibilities for distortion, I believe that the hopeful attitude and the theological or ontological convictions underlying it do generate moral energy and encourage us in the pursuit of moral ends. The eschatological hope, however, can be defended only if it is held in full awareness of its ambiguities and with acknowledgment of the dialectics of the situation. Just as faith can become hardened into dogmatism, so hope can become a mere optimism, an overweening and possibly insensitive conviction that all will turn out for the best. The choice is not one between despair and optimism, and hope should certainly not be identified with optimism. This must be said, because some theologians, especially of the secularizing sort, do seem to have come close to reducing Christian hope to a brash optimism based on the achievements of secular man and hardly to be distinguished from old-fashioned theories of progress. But it is one of the most perceptive theologians of the secular, Ronald Gregor Smith, who most severely criticizes this naïve optimism: "The countless individuals who have suffered, the great anonymous host of sufferers of torments at the hands of men, of injustice, of misery, of meaninglessness, of pain of body and agony of spirit, are a cloud of witnesses who point the finger of scorn upon all the neat and tidy optimisms which try to sweep all this accumulation of suffering under the carpet. . . . The philosophy of progress is not a Christian concept."[21]

A hope is precisely a hope, and it has the same kind of vulnerability that belongs to faith. Moreover, as far as the eschatological hope is concerned, we have to remember the dialectic of grace and endeavor. The hope is not fulfilled automatically, but only as men give themselves up in hope for its realization. Perhaps the center of the hope is simply this: that man will never find himself in an absolute *cul-de-sac;* there will always be the possibility of an opening to a new future, always the possibility that grace will transmute folly and death into atonement and resurrection.

Such an understanding of hope makes it a powerful energizing force for moral and social aspirations. But to prevent it from lapsing into complacency or giving rise to an insensitive optimism, it is necessary to remember the vulnerability of hope and to let it be continually exposed and tested in the face of all that counts against hope. And this may mean finally that perhaps only those who have been in the depths and have risen from them should be allowed to talk about hope—such talk comes too glibly from the rest of us.

One of the most impressive testimonies to hope is provided by Ulrich Simon's book *A Theology of Auschwitz.* Some have said that it is impossible to believe in God after Auschwitz. This is not Simon's conclusion, but he does take the view that we cannot turn our backs on Auschwitz, and that our beliefs and hopes are worth little unless we bring them into confrontation with the madness and monstrousness of Auschwitz and at least come to terms with it (if one may even speak in this way). "Theology speaks of eternal light, Auschwitz perpetuates the horror of darkness. Nevertheless, as light and darkness are complementary in our experience, and as the glory and the shame must be apprehended together, so the momentous outrage of Auschwitz cannot be allowed to stand, as it has done, in an isolation such as the leprous outcast used to inspire in the past."[22] Simon goes on to trace a parallel between the events of Auschwitz and the events of the passion of Jesus Christ—betrayal, arrest, trial (or whatever passes for a trial), arrival at the place of execution, and so on. The rejection and crucifixion of Christ could be regarded as the great surd of history, the proof of its essential meaninglessness and godlessness, and so of its final hopelessness. Christianity is not unaware of absurdity—it has produced its Kierkegaard, as atheism has produced its Camus. But somehow the death and suffering of Christ is transmuted into the *felix culpa*. The cross is interpreted as atonement, and alongside death is set the symbol of resurrection. Christians claim that even in the most shattering events of history our human actions intermesh with the action of God, and that he is always ahead of us (transcendent) to open up new beginnings and new possibilities of life. This is the eschatological hope. It is in some such way that Ulrich Simon can still hope and believe after Auschwitz. "The lasting significance of Auschwitz for humanity lies in its disclosure of the human condition as something incomprehensible in merely human terms."[23]

It seems to me that Simon is correct in his judgment. There is here a gap between Christian and humanist that cannot easily be bridged. One finds his ground of hope beyond man; the other pins all his hope on man. Yet the gap may not be quite unbridgeable. We have seen that in man himself there is transcendence and mystery, and there are forms of humanism that break out of the "closed" variety and gain an ontological perspective that is not too distant from that of Christianity and other religious faiths.

At the beginning of this book three main themes were announced for discussion; so, at the end, it is appropriate to ask how far we have advanced with each of these themes.

First, there was the question of the relation of Christian ethics to general moral ideals and endeavors. We have shown that this relation is to be understood mainly in terms of continuity and the pursuit of common goals. All morality is humanistic, in the sense that it seeks the fullest existence for man. The Christian ethic itself is fundamentally humanistic, for its criterion is Jesus Christ, understood in current christology as the "glory of man," the one whose christhood is a self-transcending manhood. But in showing these connections, we have tried to avoid two dangers—the danger of infringing the integrity of the non-Christian by representing him as some kind of crypto-believer and the danger of diluting Christianity so that it conforms to the accepted standards of the day.

Second, there was the question about the shape of a Christian ethic in our time. While acknowledging some virtues of the "new morality," we found it to be sadly lacking at many points. Hope for a renewed Christian ethic, I have held, is to be found by basing it on the nature of man and by seeking a new understanding of natural law. This method is by no means new, but it offers better prospects today for a rapprochement with non-Christians than does a christocentric approach. To put the matter in another way, the approach I commend founds ethics on the doctrine of creation rather than on the doctrine of redemption.

Finally, there was the difficult question about the relation of a religious faith to the moral life. In spite of the many ambiguities that attend this relation and in spite of the fact that it has frequently assumed harmful forms, we have seen reason to believe that the placing of morality in the context of faith can and should be beneficial. It should lend depth to moral obligation, seen as unconditioned demand, and it should encourage moral effort by relating it to an objective ground of hope. Through the instrumentality of liturgy and spirituality, the Christian faith does in fact seek to transform its theological vision into a way of life. And although we have given an affirmative answer to the question about the value of a relation between faith and morals, we do not see this as contradicting our endeavor to bring Christian and secular ethics closer together. For, in one form or another, phenomena such as sin and grace, faith and hope, are known far beyond the boundaries of an explicit theology.

Notes

1. Theology and Ethics

1. Harold Hatt, *Cybernetics and the Image of Man* (Nashville: Abingdon Press, 1968), p. 95.
2. Roger Shinn, *Tangled World* (New York: Charles Scribner's Sons, 1965), p. 3.
3. For further discussion, see pp. 34 ff.
4. H. J. Blackham, *Humanism* (London and Baltimore: Penguin Books, 1968), pp. 64 and 83.
5. Paul Oestreicher, ed., *The Christian-Marxist Dialogue* (London and New York: Macmillan, 1969), p. x.
6. Dietrich Ritschl, *Memory and Hope: An Inquiry Concerning the Presence of Christ* (London and New York: Macmillan, 1967), p. 190.
7. Oestreicher, *op. cit.*, p. 7.
8. Blackham, *op. cit.*, p. 128.
9. See, e.g., my inaugural lecture at Union Theological Seminary, "How is Theology Possible?" in my *Studies in Christian Existentialism* (London: S.C.M. Press; Philadelphia: Westminster Press; Montreal: McGill University Press, 1965), pp. 3–16.
10. Ludwig Feuerbach, *The Essence of Christianity*, tr. George Eliot (New York: Harper & Row, 1957), p. 274.
11. Blackham, *op. cit.*, p. 43.
12. Schubert Ogden, *The Reality of God* (New York: Harper & Row, 1966), p. 41.
13. See pp. 137 ff.

2. Problems of the New Morality

1. Bernard Häring, *Das Gesetz Christi*, 8th rev. ed., 3 vols. (Munich: Erich Wewel Verlag, 1967); Eng. tr. by G. Kaiser of 3d ed., 3 vols. (Westminster, Md.: Newman Press, 1963–66).
2. Cf. *Conscience and Its Problems* (London and New York: Longmans Green, 1927); *The Vision of God* (same publishers, 1931).
3. James M. Gustafson, "Context Versus Principles: A Misplaced Debate in Christian Ethics," *New Theology No. 3*, ed. Martin E. Marty and Dean G. Peerman (New York: Macmillan, 1966), pp. 69–102.
4. Luke 14:5.
5. John Salmond, *Jurisprudence* (London: Sweet & Maxwell, 8th ed., 1930), p. 91.
6. Aristotle, *Nicomachean Ethics*, V, 10.
7. Cf. my *Studies in Christian Existentialism*, Ch. V, "Selfhood and Temporality," pp. 58–76.
8. Norbert Wiener, *Cybernetics* (Cambridge, Mass.: M.I.T. Press, 1961), p. 121.
9. Paul Ramsey, *Deeds and Rules in Christian Ethics* (New York: Scribner, 1967), p. 20.
10. See p. 13.
11. Georg W. F. Hegel, *The Phenomenology of Mind*, tr. J. B. Baillie (London: Allen & Unwin, 1931), p. 398.
12. David Edwards, *Religion and Change* (London: Hodder & Stoughton; New York: Harper & Row, 1969), p. 314.
13. Thomas C. Oden, *Radical Obedience: The Ethics of Rudolf Bultmann* (Philadelphia: Westminster Press, 1964), p. 133.
14. John A. T. Robinson, *Honest to God* (London: S.C.M. Press; Philadelphia: Westminster Press, 1963), p. 115.
15. Ramsey, *op. cit.*, p. 22.
16. John A. T. Robinson, *Christian Morals Today* (London: S.C.M. Press; Philadelphia: Westminster Press, 1964), p. 16.
17. Joseph Fletcher, *Situation Ethics: The New Morality* (Philadelphia: Westminster Press; London: S.C.M. Press, 1966), p. 17.
18. Bernard Häring, *Shalom: Peace* (New York: Farrar, Straus & Giroux, 1967), p. 47.
19. *The Situation Ethics Debate*, ed. Harvey G. Cox (Philadelphia: Westminster Press, 1968), p. 67.
20. Fletcher, *op. cit.*, p. 98.
21. James A. Pike, *You and the New Morality* (New York: Harper & Row, 1967), pp. 70–73.

22. Paul Lehmann, *Ethics in a Christian Context* (London: S.C.M. Press; New York: Harper & Row, 1963), pp. 74 ff.
23. See p. 35.
24. See p. 84.
25. Robinson, *Christian Morals Today*, p. 20.
26. Fletcher, *op. cit.*, p. 19.
27. Karl Rahner, *The Christian of the Future*, tr. W. J. O'Hara (New York: Herder & Herder, 1967), p. 43.

3. Ethics and the New Man

1. The following list is a small selection of some of the more interesting recent books on man, and they show also something of the range of images: Pierre Teilhard de Chardin, *The Phenomenon of Man*, tr. Bernard Wall (London: Collins; New York: Harper & Row, 1959); Paul Ricoeur, *Fallible Man*, tr. Charles Kelbley (Chicago: Henry Regnery, 1965); Abraham J. Heschel, *Who Is Man?* (Stanford, Calif.: Stanford University Press, 1965); Desmond Morris, *The Naked Ape: A Zoologist's Study of the Human Animal* (New York: McGraw-Hill, 1967); Roger L. Shinn, *Man: The New Humanism* (Philadelphia: Westminster Press; London: Lutterworth Press, 1968); Harold E. Hatt, *Cybernetics and the Image of Man* (Nashville: Abingdon Press, 1968); Ray L. Hart, *Unfinished Man and the Imagination* (New York: Herder & Herder, 1968).
2. Heschel, *op. cit.*, p. 7.
3. *Ibid.*
4. Henri Bergson, *Creative Evolution*, tr. Arthur Mitchell (London: Macmillan, 1928), p. 148.
5. This is the subtitle of McLuhan's book *Understanding Media* (New York: New American Library, 1964).
6. *Lambeth Essays on Faith*, ed. A. M. Ramsey (London: S.P.C.K., 1969), p. 64.
7. See pp. 85 ff.
8. I John 3:2.
9. Martin Heidegger, *Being and Time*, tr. J. Macquarrie and E. S. Robinson (London: S.C.M. Press; New York: Harper & Row, 1962), p. 74.
10. In a lecture given at Union Theological Seminary, New York, February, 1969.
11. See pp. 82 ff.
12. Feuerbach, *op. cit.*, p. 91.

13. Genesis 2:7.
14. Dietrich Bonhoeffer, *Ethics,* tr. Neville Horton Smith (London: S.C.M. Press, 1955), pp. 84 ff.
15. Mark 10:25.
16. Allan Galloway, *Faith in a Changing Culture* (London: Allen & Unwin, 1967), p. 47.
17. Paul Ricoeur, *The Symbolism of Evil,* tr. Emerson Buchanan (New York: Harper & Row, 1967), p. 287.
18. Martin Buber, *I and Thou,* tr. Ronald Gregor Smith (Edinburgh: T. & T. Clark; New York: Charles Scribner's Sons, 2d edition, 1958), p. 3.
19. Genesis 2:18.
20. Feuerbach, *op. cit.,* p. 92.
21. Matthew 5:8.
22. William Temple, *Nature, Man and God* (London: Macmillan, 1940), p. 57.
23. John Macmurray, *The Self as Agent* (London: Faber & Faber, 1957), p. 84.
24. *Marx and Engels on Religion,* ed. Reinhold Niebuhr (New York: Schocken Books, 1964), p. 72.
25. Rudolf Bultmann, *Gnosis,* tr. J. R. Coates (London: A. & C. Black, 1952), p. 17.
26. Hegel, *op. cit.,* p. 340.
27. See p. 12.
28. James H. Cone, *Black Theology and Black Power* (New York: Seabury Press, 1969), p. 6.
29. Cf. my *Principles of Christian Theology* (New York: Charles Scribner's Sons; London: S.C.M. Press, 1966), pp. 310–12.
30. James M. Somerville, *Total Commitment: Blondel's L'Action* (Washington: Corpus Books, 1968), p. 291.
31. See Galatians 4:1–9.
32. *Das Gesetz Christi,* Vol. I, pp. 86 ff.
33. Fritz Buri, *How Can We Still Speak Responsibly of God?* tr. Charles D. Hardwick (Philadelphia: Fortress Press, 1968), p. 27.
34. *Ibid.*
35. Genesis 1:28.
36. Ulrich Simon, *A Theology of Auschwitz* (London: V. Gollancz, 1967), p. 158.
37. Galatians 4:6.
38. Shinn, *Man: The New Humanism,* p. 170.
39. *"L'amor che move il sole e l'altre stelle"*—the last line of Dante's *Divine Comedy.*

40. Sten Stenson, *Sense and Nonsense in Religion* (Nashville: Abingdon Press, 1969), p. 214.
41. Wolfhart Pannenberg, *Jesus—God and Man* (London: S.C.M. Press, 1968), pp. 83 ff.

4. Rethinking Natural Law

1. *Christian Ethics and Contemporary Philosophy*, ed. Ian T. Ramsey (London: S.C.M. Press, 1966), pp. 382–96.
2. Dietrich Bonhoeffer, *Letters and Papers from Prison*, tr. Reginald H. Fuller (New York: Macmillan, 1962), pp. 222–23.
3. See p. 40.
4. Ephesians 4:13.
5. Karl Rahner, *Theological Investigations*, Vol. I, tr. Cornelius Ernst, O.P. (London: Darton, Longman & Todd; Baltimore: Helicon Press, 1961), p. 184.
6. David Jenkins, *The Glory of Man* (London: S.C.M. Press; New York: Scribner, 1967).
7. *Ibid.*, p. 79.
8. Cf. Hebrews 1:3.
9. Matthew 13:45–46.
10. Paul Ramsey, *Basic Christian Ethics* (London: S.C.M. Press, 1953), p. 86.
11. Lehmann, *op. cit.*, p. 148.
12. See pp. 119 ff.
13. Cf. Sir Charles Sherrington, *Man on His Nature* (London: Cambridge University Press, 1940).
14. Theodosius Dobzhansky, *The Biology of Ultimate Concern* (New York: New American Library, 1967), p. 86.
15. Werner Jaeger, *The Theology of the Early Greek Philosophers*, tr. E. S. Robinson (London: Oxford University Press, 1967), p. 36.
16. *Ibid.*, pp. 115–16. Translation of Heraclitus from Jaeger.
17. *Rhetoric*, I, 10. Translation from *The Basic Works of Aristotle*, ed. Richard McKeon (New York: Random House, 1941), p. 1359.
18. Cicero, *De Republica*, III, 22–23. Translation from John Salmond, *Jurisprudence* (London: Sweet & Maxwell, 1930), p. 28.
19. *Summa Theologiae*, II/I, 91, 2. Translation from *Basic Writings of St. Thomas Aquinas*, ed. A. C. Pegis (New York: Random House, 1945), Vol. II, p. 750.
20. Richard Hooker, *Of the Laws of Ecclesiastical Polity*, I, vii, 3

(London: J. M. Dent, Everyman's Library, 1907), Vol. I, pp. 176–77.

21. John Locke, *The Reasonableness of Christianity*, ed. Ian T. Ramsey (London: A. & C. Black, 1958), p. 70.

22. Vernon J. Bourke, "Natural Law," *A Dictionary of Christian Ethics*, ed. John Macquarrie (London: S.C.M. Press; Philadelphia: Westminster Press, 1967), pp. 224–25.

23. Sophocles, *Antigone*, 450–57. Translation from *The Complete Greek Drama*, ed. Whitney J. Oates and Eugene O'Neill (New York: Random House, 1938), Vol. I, p. 434.

24. Acts 5:29.

25. E. L. Mascall, *He Who Is* (London: Darton, Longman & Todd, new edition, 1966), p. 122.

26. Ian Henderson, *Power without Glory: A Study in Ecumenical Politics* (London: Hodder & Stoughton, 1967), pp. 94–95.

27. See p. 95.

28. Buri, *op. cit.*, p. 14.

29. It may be noted that both Buri and Bultmann in their writing seem to come near to interpreting the meaning of the word "God" as that unconditioned or ultimate element which we experience in the awareness of moral obligation. This seems to reverse the traditional procedure, by deriving an understanding of God from morality rather than morality from an idea of God.

30. *Summa Theologiae*, II/I, 94, 1.

31. See p. 37.

32. Herbert Richardson has recently claimed that the Sabbath does belong to natural law, because it is related to the creation story and the "rest" of the seventh day. "This explanation of the commandment must be interpreted as implying that the Sabbath is binding not only upon Israel but also upon all other creatures. . . . it is in the same category as the commandment not to murder—it is a universal moral law." *Toward an American Theology* (New York: Harper & Row, 1967), p. 114.

33. David Ross, *The Right and the Good* (Oxford: Clarendon Press, 1930), p. 19.

34. Christopher Mooney, *Teilhard de Chardin and the Mystery of Christ* (London: Collins, 1966), p. 51.

35. See p. 92.

36. See p. 94.

37. Patrick Nowell-Smith, *Ethics* (London: Penguin Books, 1954), p. 18.

38. Cf. Mark 8:35.
39. Matthew 5:17.
40. W. D. Davies, *The Sermon on the Mount* (London and New York: Cambridge University Press, 1966), p. 29.

5. Conscience, Sin, and Grace

1. Romans 2:14–15.
2. Sigmund Freud, *An Outline of Psychoanalysis*, tr. James Strachey (London: Hogarth Press, 1949), pp. 3–4.
3. Heidegger, *op. cit.*, p. 314.
4. Friedrich Nietzsche, *The Will to Power: An Attempted Transvaluation of All Values*, tr. Anthony M. Ludovici (Edinburgh: T. N. Foulis, 1909), Vol. I, p. 226.
5. *Butler's Works*, ed. W. E. Gladstone (Oxford: Clarendon Press, 1896), Vol. II, pp. 121–35.
6. See pp. 60 ff.
7. Romans 7:15–19.
8. W. G. Maclagan, *The Theological Frontier of Ethics* (London: Allen & Unwin, 1961).
9. *Ibid.*, p. 29.
10. *Ibid.*, p. 111.
11. Cf. my *Principles of Christian Theology* (New York: Scribner's; London: S.C.M. Press, 1966), p. 245.
12. See p. 87.
13. Ricoeur, *The Symbolism of Evil*, p. 156.
14. Philippians 2:12–13.
15. See p. 51.
16. Paul Ricoeur's book *The Symbolism of Evil*, which has been quoted several times, contains a masterly analysis of the fundamental ways in which men have experienced sin.
17. Fletcher, *op. cit.*, p. 156.
18. John Baillie, *The Sense of the Presence of God* (London: Oxford University Press; New York: Scribner, 1962), p. 36.
19. See p. 50.
20. John A. T. Robinson, *Exploration into God* (Stanford, Calif.: Stanford University Press, 1967), p. 73.
21. *Ibid.*, p. 66.
22. H. J. Paton, *The Modern Predicament* (London: Allen & Unwin, 1955), p. 334.
23. *Ibid.*, p. 334.

6. Hope and the Moral Dynamic

1. I Corinthians 13:13.
2. *Summa Theologiae*, II/I, 62, 1.
3. Cf. Anders Nygren, *Agape and Eros,* tr. Philip S. Watson (London: S.P.C.K., 1937).
4. See p. 39.
5. Jürgen Moltmann, *Theology of Hope,* tr. James W. Leitch (London: S.C.M. Press; New York: Harper & Row, 1967), p. 288.
6. Chardin, *The Phenomenon of Man,* p. 231.
7. Feuerbach, *op. cit.,* p. 236.
8. Cf. my *Principles of Christian Theology,* pp. 70 ff.; also Schubert M. Ogden, *The Reality of God* (New York: Harper & Row; London: S.C.M. Press, 1967), p. 37.
9. Moltmann, *op. cit.,* p. 20.
10. I Corinthians 13:7.
11. Emil Brunner, *Faith, Hope and Love,* tr. Hugh Vernon White (Philadelphia: Westminster Press, 1956), p. 13.
12. Regin Prenter, *Creation and Redemption,* tr. Theodore I. Jensen (Philadelphia: Fortress Press, 1967), p. 202.
13. II Corinthians 5:17; Galatians 6:2; Ephesians 4:13.
14. I John 4:8.
15. Jean-Paul Sartre, *Being and Nothingness,* tr. Hazel E. Barnes (New York: Philosophical Library, 1956), p. 627.
16. Albert Camus, *The Rebel: An Essay on Man in Revolt,* tr. Anthony Bower (New York: Random House, 1956), p. 23.
17. See p. 23.
18. Walter Rauschenbusch, *Christianity and the Social Crisis* (New York: Macmillan, 1907), pp. 153–54.
19. John C. Bennett, *Foreign Policy in Christian Perspective* (New York: Scribner's, 1966), p. 105.
20. See p. 134.
21. Ronald Gregor Smith, *Secular Christianity* (London: Collins, 1966), p. 127.
22. Simon, *op. cit.,* p. 9.
23. *Ibid.,* p. 27.

Index

Action, 67 ff.
Affluence, 58 ff.
Agape, 39, 66, 133, 136
Alienation, 124 ff.
Anaximander, 92
Antinomianism, 35
Aristotle, 32, 93 f., 104, 148, 151
Arnold, Matthew, 32, 80, 128
Asceticism, 56 f.
Augustine, St., 68, 120
Authority, 22, 26

Baillie, John, 127, 153
Barth, Karl, 19, 120
Bennett, John C., 39, 140, 154
Berdyaev, N., 64
Bergson, Henri, 47, 149
Black power, 70
Blackham, Harold J., 15, 17, 23, 147
Blondel, Maurice, 71
Body, 53 f.
Bonhoeffer, D., 57, 59, 72, 83, 150, 152
Bourke, Vernon J., 99, 152
Brunner, Emil, 120, 135, 154
Buber, Martin, 31, 61, 64, 150
Bultmann, Rudolf, 69, 150, 152
Buri, Fritz, 73 ff., 102, 150, 152
Butler, Joseph, 116, 153

Calvin, J., 120
Camus, Albert, 23, 98, 138 f., 144, 154
Casuistry, 30 f., 41
Change, 52, 107
Chastity, 26 f., 48, 64
Cicero, 94, 99
Concupiscence, 59
Cone, James H., 70, 150
Conscience, 28 f., 36, 111 ff.
Contraception, 11, 47 f.
Coreth, E., 50
Cox, Harvey, 148
Creation, 55, 64, 122, 136

Davies, W. D., 110, 153
Decalogue, 100, 104 f.
Decision, 11 f., 87 f.
Descartes, R., 54, 67 f.
Dobzhansky, Theodosius, 92, 152

Edwards, David L., 35, 40, 148
Epieikeia, 32
Equity, 31 f.
Existentialism, 32, 49, 62, 68

Faith, 135 f.; *see also* Religion
Feuerbach, Ludwig, 22, 54, 64, 68, 134, 147, 149, 154

155

Fletcher, Joseph, 28, 38 ff., 127, 148, 149, 153
Freedom, 69 ff., 118, 120
Freud, Sigmund, 61, 113, 153

Galloway, A. D., 58, 150
Garaudy, Roger, 50
Genesis, 107
Gnosticism, 55
God, kingdom of, 65
    language about, 73 f., 129
    and responsibility, 75 ff.
    vision of, 79 ff.
    will of, 100 ff.
Gogarten, F., 72
Grace, 119 ff., 136
Gustafson, J., 30, 148

Hammurabi, 100
Häring, Bernard, 28, 39, 73, 75, 148
Hart, Ray, 149
Hatt, Harold, 11, 147, 149
Hegel, G. W. F., 34, 69, 148, 150
Heidegger, Martin, 50 f., 115, 149, 153
Henderson, Ian, 101, 152
Heraclitus, 93
Heschel, A. J., 44, 46, 149
Hobbes, Thomas, 61
Hooker, Richard, 94, 102, 151
Hope, 133 ff.
Humanism, 14 ff., 77, 87, 144 f.

Imago Dei, 44, 87, 91, 108, 122
Incarnation, 56
Individualism, 34, 62 ff.
Irenaeus, St., 65

Jaeger, Werner, 93, 152
Jenkins, David, 86, 152
Jesus Christ, and ethics, 16 ff., 89
    and humanity, 84 ff., 109

Kant, Immanuel, 118
Kierkegaard, S., 144
Kingdom of God, 65
Kirk, Kenneth E., 28
Knowledge, 13, 69, 74 f., 118

Law, 28 f., 32, 73, 93, 98 ff., 110; *see also* Natural law

Legalism, 28 ff., 41
Lehmann, Paul L., 28, 40, 84 ff., 91, 149, 152
Lewis, C. S., 124
Locke, John, 96, 152
Lonergan, Bernard, 50
Love, 16 f., 19, 30, 37, 66, 70, 88, 132 f., 136

Maclagan, W. G., 120 f., 153
McLuhan, Marshall, 47, 63, 68, 149
Macmurray, John, 68, 150
Mahovec, Milan, 51, 124
Man, as agent, 67–72
    changing, 46–53
    embodied, 53–60
    end of, 78 ff., 94
    and ethics, 19 ff., 42, 43 ff., 85 ff., 109, 145
    extensions of, 47 f.
    functional, 33, 71
    images of, 43 ff.
    mystery of, 50, 69, 129, 144
    responsible, 72–8, 103
    social, 60–7
    and transcendence, 49 ff., 69, 144
    see also New man
Marcel, Gabriel, 53, 71
Marty, Martin E., 148
Marx, Karl, and Marxism, 14 ff., 49, 66, 68, 77, 80 f., 124, 127, 138
Mascall, Eric L., 100, 152
Merleau-Ponty, M., 53
Moltmann, J., 134, 154
Mooney, Christopher J., 107, 152
Moral theology, 19 f., 30 f., 36, 40 f., 74
Morals, Christian and secular, 13 ff., 88 f., 131
    conventional, 115
    and religion, 21 ff., 95 ff., 131 ff.
Morgenthau, H., 140 f.
Morris, D., 44, 149
Moses, 100

Natural law, 20 f., 51 f., 82–110, 135 f.

New man, 20 f., 43 ff.
  morality, 13, 17, 18, 21, 25–42, 60, 75
Niebuhr, Reinhold, 120, 150
Nietzsche, F., 115, 153
Nowell-Smith, Patrick, 109, 152
Nygren, A., 154

Oden, T., 35, 148
Oestreicher, Paul, 16, 17, 20, 147
Ogden, S. M., 23, 147
Optimism, 108, 142–3

Pannenberg, W., 81, 151
Paton, H. J., 129 f., 133, 153
Paul, St., 46, 58, 72, 95, 112 f., 117, 123, 132, 134
Paul VI, Pope, 57, 70
Peace, 65 f.
Peerman, D., 148
Persons and personhood, 33, 48, 54, 74
Peter, St., 99
Pike, James Albert, 28, 39, 148
Plato, 54
Prenter, Regin, 136, 154
Probabilism, 30 f.
Progress, 143
Prohibitions, 35, 38, 104

Race relations, 36, 63, 70, 89
Rahner, Karl, 41, 50, 85 f., 149, 152
Ramsey, A. M., 149
Ramsey, I. T., 83, 152
Ramsey, Paul, 34, 37 f., 90, 148, 152
Rauschenbusch, W., 140, 154
Reconciliation, 16
Religion and morals, 21 ff., 95 ff., 131 ff.
Responsibility, 72 ff., 103
Resurrection, 56
Richardson, Herbert, 152
Ricoeur, Paul, 59, 122, 149, 150, 153
Ritschl, Dietrich, 17, 147
Robinson, John A. T., 28, 36 ff., 41, 104, 129, 148, 149, 153

Ross, Sir W. D., 105, 152
Rousseau, J. J., 61
Rules, 33, 35, 36, 37 f., 74, 104

Salmond, Sir John, 147
Sartre, J.-P., 50, 53, 118, 138, 154
Science, 11 f., 26, 72
Secularity, 55, 58 f., 72, 142 f.
Sermon on the Mount, 110
Sex and sexuality, 26 f., 36, 47 f., 64 f.
Sherrington, Sir Charles, 152
Shinn, Roger L., 12, 36, 77, 147, 149, 150
Simon, Ulrich, 75 f., 143 f., 150, 154
Sin, 91, 119 ff.
Situation ethics, 13, 32 ff., 38 ff.
Smith, R. G., 143, 154
Social contract, 61
  virtues, 65 f.
Somerville, J. M., 150
Sophocles, 99, 152
Space exploration, 11, 77
Stalin, Joseph, 16, 18
Stenson, Sten H., 81, 151
Subjectivism, 34
Superego, 113 f.
Superman, 76, 102, 115
Syneresis, 111

Technology, 11, 26, 57, 72, 76
Teilhard de Chardin, P., 107, 134, 149, 154
Temple, William, 67 f., 150
Theology and ethics, 15 ff., 19 ff.
Thomas Aquinas, St., and Thomism, 50, 68, 94, 100, 104, 108, 132, 152
Transcendence, 50 f., 59, 80 f.

Virtues, social, 65 f.
  theological, 131 ff.
Vision of God, 79 f.

West, Charles C., 49
Wiener, Norbert, 33, 148